visiting
Scottish West Coast Islands

Lindsey Porter

Published by
Horizon Editions Ltd
Trading as The Horizon Press
The Oaks, Moor Farm Road West, Ashbourne, Derbyshire, DE6 1HD
Tel: (01335) 347349 Fax: (01335) 347303
email: books@thehorizonpress.co.uk

ISBN: 978-1-84306-476-3

© Lindsey Porter 2010
1st Edition

Print: Gomer Press Limited. Llandysul, Ceredigion, Wales
Design & Cartography: Mark Titterton

Front Cover: Coastal croft, Lewis **Back Cover top:** Iona village
Back middle: North East Coast, Skye **Back bottom:** Black Cuillins, Skye
page 1: Butt of Lewis. Lewis (D. Simpson) **Opposite page:** Duart Castle, Isle of Mull

Picture Credits

Shutterstock: Joe Gough front cover, 6, 8 top, 8 bottom, 9 top, 13, 26, 33, 34, 41;
David Woods 9 bottom, 10-11, 67, 68 bottom-left, 88 top-right, 92; Harley Molesworth 20, 21;
Bill McKelvie 24, 25 top, 56; Stephen Finn 25 bottom, 29, 88 top-left; point-nemo 31; Rudolf Kotulán 36-37; Chris Sargent 40; Nikki Bidgood 42 top; Tiago Jorge da Silva Estima 42 bottom;
Noden-Wilkinson 64; Chris Hawker 65, 78; Awe Inspiring Images 66, 71; Klaus Rainer Krieger 68 top, 68 middle; Richard Southall 68 bottom-right

M. Olley: 19; **Isle of Eigg Heritage Trust:** 48 both;

Mark Titterton (www.ceibagraphics.co.uk): 62, 63 ; **Ardbeg Distillery:** 69 both

Sea.fari Adventures (www.seafari.co.uk): 75 top, 72

Ron Scholes (www.landscapeheritage.co.uk): 74, 75 bottom, 80, 82, 89

Acknowledgements

Ardbeg Distillery; Colonsay Brewery; Maggie Fyffe, Eigg Heritage Trust; Shutterstock;
Michael Olley; Ron Scholes; Sea.fari Adventures; Duncan Simpson

---

DISCLAIMER

Contents

Scottish YHA

☎ 0845 293 7373 (Reservations)
Has youth hostels at Lewis (2); Harris (1); Berneray (1); S. Uist (1); Skye (4); Raasay (1); Mull (1, plus nearby Oban); Islay (1); and Arran (1).
Four of the Outer Hebridean hostels are run by the Gatliff Hostels Trust. This group run simple hostels in superb locations but do not operate a reservations system. However you are unlikely to be turned away.
Visit www.gatliff.org.uk for more information.

Clisham, Harris

The nation's economic problems have caused a significant increase in the number of people holidaying in the UK at the expense of perhaps a warmer overseas destination.

Scotland will hopefully see an upturn in visitor numbers as a result of this. It undoubtedly has some of the finest scenery in the nation. If that was not enough in itself, it has the additional advantage of its archipelago of islands off the west coast.

They combine unspoilt scenery, beaches, mountains and flower-rich mochair grassland with lots of interesting wildlife and marine life. Many species are unusual elsewhere (even some unique to specific islands). Add that special quality reserved to small islands everywhere and Scotland is lucky to have such a wonderful tourism bonus just off the mainland coast.

Favoured by the Gulf Stream, it brings warm waters and a higher incidence of sun than one might expect. This mix of special features has already been recognised in some of the islands, especially those within easy reach of the mainland eg Skye, Mull, Arran and Bute. Even the Outer Hebrides and Islay have become much more popular despite a longer sea voyage.

I hope that this book helps to promote tourism especially to the less visited islands. To this end, accommodation details are more extensive on the smaller islands, rather than just quoting the Tourist Information Centre booking agency phone number. Likewise, more of the businesses likely to be of interest to visitors (if only for the mail order opportunities) are included.

This book does not intend to give a background of island history etc. It concentrates on giving visitors details on what to see, where to go and what to do; enabling the most to be made from the planning to the actual visit.

Lewis and Harris

Outer
Hebrides

Butt of Lewis
Port Nis
Borve
Barvas
Bragair
Dun Carloway
Broad
Bay
Uig
Gt. Bernera
Stornoway
Eyre
Peninsula
Gallernish
Stones
Mealista
Crossbost
Lewis
Ullapool
Scarp
Loch Resort
Loch Seaforth
Clisham
Tarransay
Tarbert
Harris
Scalpay
The
Minch
Luskentyre
Beach
Northton
Pabbay
Leverburgh
Uig (Skye)
Berneray
Ferry
Sound
of Harris
N. Uist
Isle of Skye

N
W   E
S

Lewis

The Outer Hebrides or Western Isles are a roughly north-south orientated chain off the north west coast of Scotland. The largest island, Lewis & Harris is the more northerly, being some 80 miles (128km) long and 14 miles (22km) wide. However, the road journey is more tortuous and longer, especially travelling from east to west. The landmass extends to over 800 sq miles (2,072 sq km). To the north of the Western Isles chain is the island of North Rona, which is now an uninhabited island nature reserve. This is also described in this section.

The Outer Hebrides

Dun Carloway, Isle of Lewis

Although often thought, and even referred to, as an island. Harris is not an island and consists of the bottom 1/3rd of an island where the other 2/3rds are known as the Isle of Lewis.

Harris may have a small neck of land joining it to Lewis, but physically the range of mountains running across the south of Lewis created a barrier as effective as the sea itself. Here the mountains rise up to 2,622ft (799m). To the north, the rest of Lewis is below 1,000ft (305m) and dotted with numerous small lochs. Much of this area is under a blanket of peat, laid down since the first settlers came here. The link with these early times is impressive with the Callanish Standing Stones, on the north coast near to Callanish, of international importance. There are remains of Iron Age houses and the tallest standing stone in Scotland

This largest of the Western Isles has successfully kept the excesses of our modern day culture in check. It has preserved peace and quiet, Sunday observance and the Gaelic language. It also embraces some commercialism but it is fitting that its greatest product, Harris Tweed, is based upon sustainability, even if demand now sees the island importing wool from the mainland.

Mangurstadh Beach, Isle of Lewis

Stone Circle at Callanish, Isle of Lewis

The unusual architecture of Stornoway Town Hall in Lewis

Stornoway is the only town in the Western Isles (or Outer Hebrides) that is able to cater for the needs of most visitors, but beware the almost universal shutdown on Sundays, for which visitors need to be prepared (see below), an important exception being the ferries. Since 20th July 2009, CalMac have operated a Sunday service between the Scottish mainland (Ullapool) and Stornoway.

The island is particularly scenic with white-shell sand predominating on the Atlantic side. Here are beautiful expanses of sand, largely devoid of people. On one of these, in 1831 at Ardroil near Uig, a stone chamber was found, previously hidden under the sand on the edge of the beach. It was revealed following a very high tide and gale-force winds which removed a lot of sand. It gave up 93 chess pieces made from the ivory of walrus teeth and of Viking provenance (c. 1140-1160AD). On the opposite coast, the shoreline consists of fingers of land jutting into the sea; a completely different coastline, but equally as endearing.

Great Bernera

The largest island in Loch Roag and joined by a bridge to Lewis in 1953. It is c. 6 miles/9.5km x 3 miles/5km wide. In the island's centre is the village of Breacleit, with a shop, post office and café in the large community centre. The Bernera Museum is also here. Fishing and lobster catching is a local occupation, especially the latter, from Kirkibost.

Surviving Sunday

As stated above, the islanders observe Sunday and most places are closed. There are churches belonging to the United Free Church, the Free Church of Scotland, the Church of Scotland, the Free Presbyterian Church and the Roman Catholic Church. They all welcome visitors to their services. However, the Sunday morning service (11am or noon) is generally in Gaelic. The evening service (6pm or 7pm) is in English.

In Stornoway, the hotels are generally open on Sundays, but some B & B's do not take visitors on a Sunday. The only garage in

A panorama of Seilebost Beach on a showery day, South Harris

Stornoway to open is Englebrets opposite the Western Isles offices. Many attractions are closed (such as museums and sports facilities, even some of the parks and most toilets. Those in the centre of Stornoway offer a much needed comfort zone.

Sunday has to be prepared for; sort out your food and accommodation; if travelling by car, check the fuel tank. A car trip may be a good idea and remember that the Doune Braes Hotel in the west is usually open. If you are thinking of using the airport bus on a Sunday, you are out of luck.

Harris

The part of the island known as Harris consists of the mountainous area south of Lewis, with a northern boundary running roughly from Loch Reasort in the west to Loch Shiphoirt in the east. Until a road was blasted through the mountains, the area to the south developed in isolation from Lewis.

The geography is a little different, supporting less fertile soils, especially in the east. The Gaelic dialect is different from Lewis; it is softer and with less Norse words in the language. If not an island in the true sense, it developed as if it was one and retains its separate identity. It is known as the Isle of Harris too.

The 'capital' is really a village, Tarbert, the destination for the Uig ferry from Skye. Unlike Lewis, there is little industry in Harris and high unemployment as a result, despite some initiatives. Tourism plays a key part in the economy, but it is seasonal as well as suffering the vagaries of recent UK summers. None the less it is a gem in terms of its attractive scenery, empty landscapes and memorable as well as empty beaches.

Lord Leverhume purchased the south Harris estate in the 1920s and sunk a lot of money into the island, especially at An t-Ob, now Leverburgh, where the North Uist ferry docks. However, the stimulus ended with his death and Leverburgh did not develop like Stornoway to the north.

The local economy at Leverburgh received a good boost when the ferry from here to North Uist commenced in 1996.

Like Lewis its coastline consists of impressive shell-sand beaches on the Atlantic coast and an indented coastline on the south east coastline. The Sound of Harris between Harris and North Uist is the only deep water channel between islands of the Outer Hebrides. There are a significant number of crofts on the island and sheep's wool is used locally for Harris Tweed manufacture.

By contrast, the mountains bordering Lewis rise to a significant height. The highest being Clisham at 2,622ft/799m. The mountains range north west from Clisham with at least three other peaks over 2,000ft/610m high

The mountains, on their north east side form the border with Lewis, with Loch Reasort in the north west and Loch Shiphoirt in the south east. Loch Reasort has Scarp Island at it sea-end. It is not very fertile but in 1881 supported a population of over 200. Now it is deserted. Loch Shiphoirt stretches up into Lewis to Ceann Shiphoirt, a distance in excess of 12 miles/19km.

Scalpay

Situated off the east side of Harris is another well populated island, Scalpay, which was joined to Harris by a substantial concrete-built bridge in 1997. The island is 3 miles/5km x 2 miles/3km in extent and has a population of c. 400.

The road through the mountains, the A859 has a junction at the south end with the B887 which is a narrow B-road leading to Huisinis and the island of Scarp, a distance of 15 miles/24km. Some superb scenery awaits you at Huisinis; look out for Arnhuinnsuidhe Castle on the way.

The A859 runs around the north west side of Harris close to the coast and passing the spectacular Luskentyre Beach, with the now deserted offshore island of Taransay. The beach is at its best when the adjacent machair grassland is covered by a blanket of flowers.

Taransay

Taransay, off the Atlantic coast of Harris, is now without a permanent population, for they left in the 1970s. A couple of buildings – the former school and Mackay House are now self-catering holiday cottages. The island is noted for its sandy beaches and machair meadowland and extends to 3,500ac/1416ha. It was used by the BBC for the filming of *Castaway* in 2000, when a group of people including the then unknown Ben Fogle, arrived here and were left to see what happened during the ensuing year. There is now self catering accommodation in the buildings used by the 'castaways'. (Go to www. visit-taransay.com or ☎ 07867 968560

The island itself is 3 miles/5km x 4.5 miles/7km and rises to a height of 875ft/282m. In 1901, it had a population of 72.

Fact File

Getting There

CalMac operates ferries from Ullapool to Stornoway; from Berneray on North Uist to Leverburgh on Harris and from Uig on Skye to Tarbert, Harris. The Ullapool crossing is daily. Note: the Uig –Harris service does not run on Sundays. The Berneray-Leverburgh service also runs daily.

By Air

There is an airport 3 miles (5km) east of Stornoway (☎ 01851 702256). It is open on Sundays. There are scheduled flights from Aberdeen (Eastern Airways); Benbecula (Highland);

Edinburgh (Flybe); Glasgow (Flybe) and Inverness (Flybe & Highland). The airport bus to Stornoway runs at regular intervals, daily (Mon-Sat). For information on this or booking an airport taxi, ring the Airport Info Desk on ☎ 01851 702256. For bus timetables go to: www.w-isles.gov.uk/travel/index.htm

Accommodation

The Stornoway & Harris Tourist

Information Centres have a booking service. Remember some B & B's may not take visitors for Sunday night.

26 Cromwell Street, Stornoway
☎ 01851 703088
Open all year

Tarbert Tourist Information Centre

Pier Road, Isle of Harris HS3 3DJ
☎ 01859 502011
Open April-October

Harris has two hotels: The Harris in Tarbert ☎ 01859 502154 and The Hebrides, also in Tarbert ☎ 01859 502364. There are several guest houses, B & B's and plenty of self-catering properties.

Places to Visit

Arnol Blackhouse

Arnol HS2 9DB
☎ 01851 710395

Bosta Iron Age House

Gt Bernera HS2 9LT
☎ 01851 612331
(Small island with bridge link) Reconstructed Iron Age house. Open in summer. Island has its own museum/café at Breacleit in the community centre.

Harris Mountains

Callanish Standing Stones

Loch Roag
☎ 01851 621422
www.calanaisvisitorcentre.co.uk
One of the most important megalithic sites in Europe (4,000 years old). Rows of over 50 large standing stones in a cross shape, with 7 stone circles within 4 miles/6km. Visitor Centre open in summer (not Sundays) with coffee shop, also Blackhouse tearoom.

Dun Carloway

Above Loch Roag, near Carloway
☎ 01851 643338
www.calanaisvisitorcentre.co.uk
Iron Age defensive structure, called a Dun or Broch, consisting of two concentric stone walls containing upper floors. It is an impressive 30ft/9m high x 48ft/15m diameter. Visitor Centre open in summer. This Broch, after the one on Mousa Island in the Shetland Isles is considered to be the finest in the country.

Gearrannan, Baile Tughaidh

Blackhouse Village
Arnol
☎ 01851 643416
Restored village; experience traditional rural activities, the history of the area and how people lived here in the past in the low-walled buildings called black houses.

Museum Nan Eilean, Stornoway Museum
Francis St, Stornoway
☎ 01851 709266
Outer Hebrides way of life and traditions.

Ness Heritage Centre
10 Callicot, Ness HS2 0TG
☎ 01851 810377
www.ce-n.org
Opportunity to see records, video and audio recordings; café.

St Clements Church
Rodel (Roghadal)
Thought to be 14th century and repaired in the 16th century. Includes tomb of Alexander MacLeod (died 1547), one of the finest in Scotland.

St Molvag's Church
Tabost
Also known as St Olafs. Possibly 14th century and on the site of an older cell or chapel of the 10th century.

Shawbost Norse Mill & Kiln
Shawbost HS2 9BQ
☎ 01851 710797
On the A858 nr Shawbost, by Loch Roinaval. A renovated pair of thatched buildings with a kiln producing meal from cereals (barley). Water powered grinding mill.

Steinacleit Cairn/Stone Circle
On A857 Stornoway – Ness road
South end of Loch an Duin, near Shader.

Trussell Stone
By A857, 2 miles (4km) north east of Upper Barvas
Largest single standing stone in Scotland; 20ft/6m high; no charge.

Other Attractions

An Lanntair Arts Centre
Kenneth St, Stornoway
☎ 01851 703307
www.lanntair.com
The island's art centre.

Harris Tweed & Knitwear
4 Plocropool HS3 3EB
☎ 01859 502040

Harris Tweed Shop
Caberfeidh, Tarbert HS3 3DJ
☎ 01859 502040

Harris Tweed Textiles
Carloway Mills HS2 9AG
☎ 01851 643300
Last remaining independent wholesale producers of Harris Tweed. New Visitor Centre; view processes involved in tweed production. Tweeds for sale. Coffee shop.

Hebridean Brewery Co
18a Bells Road, Stornoway HS1 2RA
☎ 01851 700123
www.hebridean-brewery.co.uk
2003 Bronze Medal, Soc., of Independent Brewers 'Beer of Scotland Premium Cask Category'.

Hebridean Soap Co
25 Breasclete, West Side HS2 9EF
☎ 01851 621206
sales@hebrideansoap.co.uk

Ian Stewart-Hargreaves Silversmith
Creaganan Gorm, Carloway HS2 9AG
☎ 01851 643356
Ian@creaganan.com

Isle of Harris Knitwear
Grosebay HS3 3EF
☎ 01859 511240

Stornoway Fish Smokers
Shell St., HS1 2BS
☎ 01851 702723
The last traditional kippering house on Lewis.

Kinloch Museum
Laxay Lochs HS2 9LA
☎ 01851 830359
Open April-Sept

Latta's Mill
North side of golf course
Rebuilt old mill; free admission.

Lewis Loom Centre
The Old Grainstore 3, Bayhead, HS1 2DU
Cromwell St, Stornoway
☎ 01851 703117/ 704500
Guided tour and demonstrations of Harris Tweed production.

Lewis Sports Centre, Stornoway
☎ 01851 709191
Open: daily (except Sunday) 8am-10pm; 9am-8pm Saturday,
Café.

MacGillivray Machair Centre
Northton (Taobh Tuath)
Learn about the machair grassland landscape with its masses of flowers.

RSPB Bird Reserve
Loch na Muilne, nr Stornoway.
A coastal reserve consisting of two small lochs, wetland and moorland.

This 'n' That
36 Point St, Stornoway
☎ 01851 702202
www.callanishjewellery.com
Locally sourced crafts and tweeds.

Whalebone Arch
A857
The lower jaw bones of a blue whale stranded in 1920 on a nearby beach. Harpoon at top of arch was still in the whale but explosive device had failed to go off. Apparently it later did so in somebody's shed!

Tours, Trips & Adventure

Adventure Hebrides
20a Coll, Back HS2 0JR
☎ 01851 820726

Albannach Guided Tours
1 Tomair, Balallan, Lochs HS2 9PP
☎ 01851 830433
www.albannachtours.co.uk
sales@albannachtours.co.uk

Hebridean Challenge
4a Brocair, Point HS1 0EZ
☎ 01851 870716

Island Cruising
1 Erista, Uig HS2 9JG
☎ 01851 672381

Lewis Boat Trip
Stornoway
☎ 01851 702304/ 07766 375434
www.visithebrides.co.uk
Behind lifeboat station.

Out & About Tours
25 Valasay, Gt. Bernera HS2 0XP
☎ 0851 612288

Seatrek
☎ 01851 672464
www.seatrek.co.uk
Boat trips around Uig coast and beyond. One or two-hour trips. Also adventure packages eg sea kayaking,

rock climbing/abseilling. New boat, offering capacity for 12 passengers, for day hire on west coast of Scotland.

Sea Harris
East Tarbert, Harris HS3 3DB
☎ 01859 502007/07760 216555
www.seaharris.co.uk
Trips to St Kilda.

Cycle Hire
Alex Dans Cycle Hire
67 Kenneth St, Stornoway
☎ 01851 704025

Harris Cycle Hire
2 Glen Kyles
Leverburgh HS5 3TY
☎ 01859 520319

Golf
Stornoway Golf Club
Lady Lever Park, Stornoway HS2 0XP
☎ 01851 702240

Harris Golf Club
Scarista Mhor
☎ 01859 550331

General Store/Fuel
Engebrets
Opposite Western Isles Offices, Stornoway
Convenience food store and petrol station. Open daily.

Events
Lewis Highland Games
Held late-July.

Other Information
Scottish Natural Heritage
32 Francis St, Stornoway HS1 2ND
☎ 01851 705258

Car Hire
Lewis Car Rents
52 Bayhead St, Stornoway
☎ 01851 703760
www.lewis-car-rental.com

Stornoway Car Hire
☎ 01851 702658
www.stornowaycarhire.co.uk

North Rona

North Rona is the most northerly land mass in Britain although now no longer inhabited. Lying 45miles/72km north west of Cape Wrath (at Lat. 59° 7'30" and Long. 5° 50') it is the most northerly extent of the Outer Hebrides. It is about one mile long and one mile in width, some 300acres/ in extent. There is a ridge across the middle, which rises to a height of 348 ft/106m at Toa Rona in the south east which ends in vertical cliffs above the sea.

North Rona

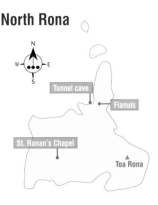

There are no landing facilities at North Rona

A flattish peninsula runs northwards called Fianuis and across the neck of it is a tunnel cave going from coast to coast with a large blow hole in the middle. The population seems to have literally died out in 1680 probably from starvation. Rats coming ashore (on flotsam) ate the corn crop and shortly afterwards the island's bull was taken by pirating seamen. Bad weather saw no boats from Lewis for a year and when Lewis men eventually made the journey, there were no survivors.

A fresh group went to North Rona but in c. 1695, most of the men were lost in a disaster. Francis Thompson in his *St Kilda & Other Hebridean Outliers* suggests this was probably the result of a boating accident. The women and remaining males were taken off as a result. The island had no beach to house boats, which were unusual here.

Two shepherds tried to make a life here in 1884 but their stay was short lived and both were found dead in April 1885. During the Great War, the German submarine U-90 stopped here to shoot sheep for mutton.

Today the island has been a National Nature Reserve since 1956. There are no permanent inhabitants. Access is difficult even in good weather. One ruined building is of special significance. It is the cell of St. Ronan, dating from the 8th century. All the buildings on Rona were half buried for protection and this was the same with the cell or chapel. Some restoration work was done in the 1930s of a sympathetic nature and it remains one of the oldest buildings in the realm, protected by isolation and an uncompromising sea.

The NNR consists of North Rona and Sula Sgeir Island, 10miles/16km to the west. North Rona supports the 3rd largest breeding colony of grey seals in the UK (5% of the annual pups bred). The 2nd largest is at Monach Islands (west of North Uist). North Rona supports 130,000 seabirds including both storm and Leach's petrel; gannet and guillemots.

Fact File

Getting There

With no ferry, you need to make your own arrangements to get there. Getting ashore is not easy. You are recommended to contact the Scottish Natural Heritage office in the first instance: 32 Francis Street, Stornoway, Isle of Lewis HS1 2ND. ☎ 01851 705258

Northern Light Charters offer a cruise to North Rona if there is sufficient demand for the trip. Contact them at Achnacraig, Achindarroch, Duror of Appin, Argyll PA38 4BS. ☎ 01631 740595 They also run Hebridean ecology holidays, sleeping for several nights on their boat and sailing around different specified islands in both the Inner and Outer Hebrides, including St. Kilda.

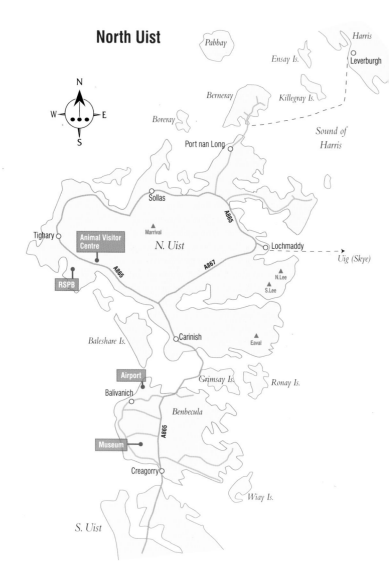

North Uist

North Uist

If you are planning a trip to the Western Isles or Outer Hebrides (both names are in common use), you have a choice of landing (by sea) in Lewis (Ullapool to Stornoway, 2 hours 45 minutes), Harris (Uig on Skye to Tarbert, 1 hour 40 minutes) or in North Uist (from Uig on Skye to Lochmaddy, 1 hour 45 minutes). If either of the first two, the ferry south from Harris (Leverburgh) takes you to Berneray on a 60-minute journey across the Sound of Harris. Now, once on Berneray, you do not need a ferry until you leave Eriskay for Barra if your journey is to explore the necklace of islands as they stretch away to the south for a total of 130 miles/208km from the north of Lewis.

The Machair at Northton, looking towards North Uist

This has been achieved by linking islands with causeways. The islands have lost some of their isolation but hopefully not their soul in the process. The first causeway unites tiny Berneray with North Uist. The latter is relatively flat with much of it covered with water. Exceptionally, the two highest hills on the island lie in the east. South Lee, reaching a height of 898ft/274m and Eaval, to the south being higher at 1,139ft/347m.

They rise like islands above a watery interior crossed by the rebuilt A867. At the north east end of this road is Lochmaddy, where the ferry from Uig on Skye docks. It is the main community on the island, with most services available including a hospital, if needed and a museum/art centre, plus a garage, local shopping, post office etc.

Two-thirds of North Uist probably consists of fresh water in small lakes (lochans) and peat bogs. The other third is on the west side of the island where the north-south road is situated.

Straun Thatched Roof
Cottage, Sollas, North Uist

Scolpaig Tower, North Uist.
A folly on site of a broch

Even this is circuitous in the north, having to contend with the lochans terrain. From Newtonferry, the B893 heads south west to meet the A865 to Lochmaddy.

The quickest route south is to turn left towards Lochmaddy on the A865, from there go right on the newly completed two-lane A867. The former road skirts a short range of hills. The first two (to the west) are Crogary Mor (on the left) and Maari (on the right) – actually there is another adjacent and to the east, Crogary Beag. Between the first two is a standing stone and by the A865 at the foot of Maari is the small Loch Aonghais with a dun (small fort) in the middle of it. The OS maps for the Outer Hebrides are littered with examples of both these ancient features.

A more tortuous single lane route, but arguably the more interesting, is to go right at the T-junction with the two A-roads. It leads to the small communities of Grenitote and Sollas (Co-op & post office) and hugs the south end of Valley Strand, looking out to the island of Valley. There is a causeway across it to Valley House at low tide. Heading south, Balranald is reached, with its church on the left and RSPB reserve on the right. Here wildlife thrives, especially the birds, in the sand dunes faced by a rocky foreshore with machair grasslands, marshes and more shallow lochs.

Just beyond the reserve, the road hugs the coast from Bayhead (shop) until Clachan-a-Luib (shop) is reached where the A867 goes left to Lochmaddy to complete a circuit of the north of the island. The A865 continues south with the island of Baleshare to the right. About 5miles/8km south of Bayhead is a turn to the right to access Baleshare Island, now with a causeway. Here is a small community and a large area of sand dunes, chiefly in the south of the island.

One and a half miles beyond here is the village of Carinish, with its inn and remains of Trinity Temple (Teampull na Trionaid). This consists of two church buildings, founded in c. 1200 on an earlier site, apparently by the daughter of King Robert II. From here the A865 circles round towards the sea cutting through a stone circle with a chambered cairn on the bank below and to the left. Another causeway, the North Sound Causeway, now links North Uist with Benbecula via the island of Grimsay and using several small islets as 'stepping stones' en-route. The North Sound Causeway is about 2.5 miles/4km in length and reaches Benbecula near to the airport.

Grimsay

Grimsay is approximately 3 miles/5km long x 2 miles/3km wide with a small roadside community at Baymore. It struggles to break the 66ft/20m contour height. At the south east extremity of the island are the remains of St Michaels Chapel. Beyond is another island, Ronay, with a land mass similar to Grimsay. Unlike the low-lying Grimsay, Ronay is hilly, the highest point being 377ft/115m at Beinn a Charnain.

Fact File

Getting There

By causeway from Benbecula (if driving north up the Outer Hebridean islands). To get to Benbecula, take CalMac ferry to Lochboisdale on South Uist from Oban.
From the Isle of Harris by ferry from Leverburgh to Berneray and causeway to North Uist.
Better still, direct to Lochmaddy from Uig, on Skye (1 hour 45 minutes).
CalMac, Lochmaddy ☎ 01876 500337

By Air

Glasgow to Benbecula.

Accommodation

Hotels

Langass Lodge
Lochmaddy
Grimsey Island HS6 5HA
☎ 01876 580285

Lochmaddy Hotel
Pier Road, HS6 5AA
☎ 01876 500331

Temple View Hotel
Carinish HS6 5EJ
☎ 01876 580676

Tigh Dearg Hotel
Lochmaddy
☎ 01876 500700
Has Leisure Club and sauna etc.
All four have a bar/evening meals.

Guest House

Ardnastruban House
Grimsay Island HS6 5HT
4* B & B, 3 bedrooms (double, twin, single).
☎ 01870 602452

Self Catering

Stuan Cottage
Sollas
drdmacaulay@hotmail.com
Typical thatched cottage by the sea.

Tigh-na-Mara
Claddach, Kirkibost
5* bungalow, sleeps 8 in 4 bedrooms
☎ 0871 910 6731
e: info@tigh-na-mara.biz

Also Contact:
Tourist Information Centre
Pier Road, Lochmaddy, HS6 5AA
☎ 01876 500321
Open Apr–Oct (Stornoway open all year)

Activities

Uist Outdoor Centre
Lochmaddy HS6 5AE
☎ 01876 500 480

Car Hire

MacLennans
Balivanich
☎ 01870 602191

Cycle Hire

Lochmaddy
☎ 01876 500358

Petrol

Available in Bayhead & Lochmaddy

Food

Hebridean Smokehouse
Clachan, Locheport HS6 5HD
☎ 01876 580209
Peat smoked fish/seafood

RSPB Balranald
Visitor Centre open April-August; free
admission

Benbecula

Connecting North and South Uist is
Benbecula, with a causeway at North
and South Ford respectively. The island is
6-7 miles/10-11km long and flat, with a
single hill, Rueval, reaching 407ft/124m.
It has extensive views to the north and
south. Another hill Beinn a Tuath rises to
336ft/102m on the island of Wiay, just off
the south west coast and possibly connected
to Benbecula at low tide.

Benbecula is much like North Uist and the
top part of South Uist with numerous small
lochs, (lochans) and little population, which is
concentrated on the western side of the island.
Here there are lovely sandy beaches, dunes and
mochair contrasting with sea lochs and a rugged
coastline, which characterises the east side.

Benbecula has an airport with flights from
Glasgow and Barra (operated by Loganair
for Flybe) and from Stornoway (operated by
Highland Airways). It is at Balivanich, the ad-
ministrative centre for North Uist, South Uist
and Benbecula. The island has a population of c.
1,200 and most live around or in the town.

Further south at Liniclate is the secondary
school for the Uists. It also houses the community centre, with a swimming pool, sports
facilities, café, museum and library. Just north
of South Ford causeway is Creagory, with
the Dark Island Hotel and Co-op shop. The
B891 from Liniclate heads south east linking
several small islands with causeways. However,
it stopped short of linking with Wiay Island.
The road finishes at a small pier with deeper
water than at Liniclate or Creagory.

The two main causeways are of significant
length, North Ford being 5 miles/8km and
South Ford, rebuilt in the late 1970s and
opened in 1982, is chiefly a bridge replacing
an 82-span concrete bridge built in 1942.

Fact File

Accommodation

Hotels
Isle of Benbecula House Hotel
Creagory
☎ 01870 602024
Fishing on 16 lochs

Dark Island Hotel
Liniclate
☎ 01870 603030

B & B's
Kyles Flodda, HS7 5QR
☎ 01870 603145

Creag Liath, Griminish
☎ 01870 602992

Bainbhidh, Griminish
☎ 01870 602532

Lionacleit Guest House, 27 Liniclate, Griminish ☎ 01870 602176

Borve Guest House, Griminish ☎ 01870 602685

Self Catering
Gramsdale, Griminish ☎ 01870 602536

27 Liniclate, Griminish ☎ 01870 602176

Ford House, 3 Creagorry, Griminish ☎ 01870 602239

1 Grimsay Island, Griminish ☎ 01870 602591

7 Torlum, Griminish ☎ 01870 603296

Places to Visit
Borve Castle
Left of B892 near Borve Chapel, but east of the road. A Clan Ranald Castle burned by Royalists loyal to George II

Borve Chapel ruins
Three miles (5km) south of Nunton Chapel, off road to west

Dun Buidhe
On island in Loch Dun Mhurchaidh, south east of airport. Iron Age with significant remains

Gift Shop
MacGillivrays (incl., Harris Tweed) ☎ 01870 602525

Museum Nan Eilean
Sgoil Lionacleit, Benbecula HS7 5PJ ☎ 01870 602864

Nunton Steadings, Griminish ☎ 01870 602039
"Promoting and interpreting heritage and environment in the Southern Isles"

Nunnery chapel ruins, Nunton
South of Balivanich, on the B892. 14th century chapel, destroyed during the Reformation when the nuns were massacred

Teampull Chaluim
Another chapel ruin of significant age, on B892 south of the airport

Car Hire
Ask Car Hire, Lionacleit, HS7 5PG ☎ 01870 602818

Golf
Benbecula Golf Club
Balivanich,
2 x 9-holes on machair grassland

Fishing floats washed up on the coast in Benbecula

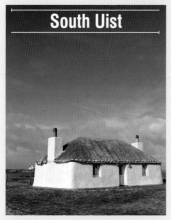

South Uist

A traditional thatched and whitewashed cottage on the Isle of South Uist

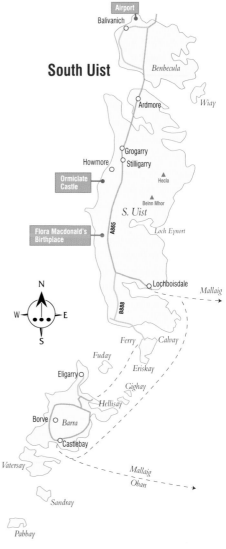

South Uist is the second largest island in the Western Isles. It is 22miles long/35km and nearly 8miles/13km in breadth. It is best described as being flat in the west, hilly in the middle and mountainous in the east. It has a large area of small lochs (lochans) in the north, west and in the south (north of Loch Boisdale). The mountains are highest in the north with Beinn Mhor at 1,922ft/586m, the highest mountain south of the North Harris range and not to be confused with Beinn Mhor on Harris, which is slightly lower.

The South Uist range also includes immediately to the north east of Beinn Mhor: Ben Corodale at 1,634ft/498m and Hecla 1,879ft/573m. Although the west coast has some lovely beaches, the north west section is off limits and marked on the O.S. map as 'Danger Area' because of the missile firing range of the M.O.D. This facility was threatened with closure in June 2009 with the loss of 125 jobs at risk and the saving of £40m. In the following September, a reprieve was announced by the Government. It would also have affected the tracking station on St Kilda. The episode highlighted the fragile nature of the outer islands' economy.

Approached from the South Ford bridge in the north, the A865 runs due south (virtually) for most of the island and then goes to the south east to Lochboisdale. Here the ferry leaves for Castlebay on Barra or Oban on the mainland. This is the main area of population on the island. Most of the services available on South Uist may be found here in addition to other village facilities.

Continuing south, the road is the B888 heading for West Kilbride. Here a minor road heads along the coast through East Kilbride to Ludag, where a causeway now links South Uist with Eriskay Island, from where there is a ferry to Barra. There are many spur roads leading off the A865 to the west and east, which allow a better exploration of the island.

Fact File

Getting There

Road from Benbecula and and ferry from Mallaig; Oban (Via Barra) (mainland Scotland) or Castlebay, Barra

Loch Druidibeg, South Uist

Accommodation

Lochboisdale Hotel
Isle of S. Uist HS8 5TH
☎ 01878 700332

Orasay Inn
Lochcarnan HS8 5PD
☎ 01870 610298

Borrodale Inn
Daliburgh HS8 5SS
☎ 01878 700444

Polochar Inn
West Kilbride, Lochboisdale HS8 5TT
☎ 01878 700215

South Uist has a range of other accommodation options – contact Tourist Information.

Tourist Information Centre
Lochboisdale ☎ 01878 700286
Open: Easter to October. In winter contact TIC at Stornoway on Lewis.

Places to Visit

Flora Macdonald's Birthplace
Now a ruin off the A865, southwest of Kildonan School at Milton.

Howmore Church
An historic village with ruins of 12th and 13th century chapels. In the centre of the church is an unusual communion pew.

Kildonan Museum
Kildonan HS8 5SQ
☎ 01878 710343,
Museum/Arts Centre

Loch Druidibeg, National Nature Reserve
☎ 01870 620238
Adjacent to the A865 and B890
Loch, wetlands, mochair and moorland grassland habitats. Important breeding place for the corncrake and greylag goose (May-June) and mochair flowers in July.

Ormacleit Castle
Castle ruin west of A865 near village of same name. Built in 1701 by Chief of Clan Ranald, but destroyed by fire in early 18th Century, possibly because of Clan Ranald's involvement with the 1715 Old Pretender's rebellion. Substantial remains survive.

Our Lady of the Isles Statue
In the north of the island by the A865 is a huge statue 125ft/38m high.

Cycle Hire

Rothan Cycles
9 Howmore, S. Uist HS8 5SH
☎ 01870 620283

Golf

Askernish Golf Club
Askernish HS8 5SS
☎ 07900 387167

Shopping

Salar Smokehouse
The Pier, Lochcarnan HS8 5PD
☎ 01870 610324

Craft Shop
Kildonan Centre HS8 5RZ
☎ 01870 620380

Scottish Natural Heritage
Stilligarry HS8 5RS
☎ 01870 620238

Monach Isles

National Nature Reserve, Scottish Natural Heritage

☎ 01870 620238

Five islands off the west coast. Important breeding colony of Atlantic grey seals and large numbers of sea birds. Best time to visit is May-August. No visitor facilities

Contact Tourist Information or seek advice from Scottish National Heritage on the above telephone no.

Eriskay

Situated off the south coast of South Uist is the island of Eriskay, its isolation ending in 2001 by the construction of a causeway from its northern neighbour. At over a mile in length, it also carries the island's water and electricity supply. Another 'stepping stone' in the improved communication links of the Outer Herbrides came with the vehicle ferry to Barra with a new jetty from just outside Am Baile, the community on the north west corner of the island.

The island is approximately 4miles/9km x 2.5miles/4km in breadth and with a population of c.200 (or just under). It reaches a height of 606ft/185m at Beinn Scrien.

Although well known because of the wreck of the whisky-laden ship *S.S. Politician* (see below), the island has its own species of pony, which is now recovering from danger levels of extinction. It is the place where Prince Charles Edward Stuart (Bonnie Prince Charlie) landed from France on the frigate *le Duc Teillay* in 1745. He was taken to Skye from the Outer Hebrides by Flora MacDonald, who lived there, but was born on South Uist.

The Eriskay Jersey is a (chiefly blue) seamless garment with intricate patterns. Production is limited to a few ladies and the garments are comparatively rare. It is a kind of Scottish knitware now confined to Eriskay, but formerly made over a wider area.

The community of Am Baile has a shop and community centre together with the island's school and Roman Catholic church.

The *S.S. Politician*

In February 1941 this vessel, heading for the U.S.A. with a valuable cargo, intended to raise much needed sterling, ran aground off Eriskay, just to the east of Calvay. The crew were rescued and the vessel lay at the mercy of the waves before the nature of the cargo began to circulate. What followed elevated Eriskay into the realms of modern mythology, although the basic facts were true enough, what unfolded was a wrecker's dream, an Eldorado in the shape of a ship's cargo lying just beyond the shoreline.

The *S.S. Politician*, respectfully known locally as The Polly, was carrying bicycles (not seen before on Eriskay), perfume, thousands of yards of shirt lengths and whisky, lots of it. In fact there were 20,300 cases or 243,000 bottles of over-proof malt.

Men came across the sea from other islands; as many as 50 men a night toiled in seawater using the shirt lengths to lift the precious liquid out of the hold and into waiting boats. Then the Customs and Revenue arrived to search where it had gone. It still appears to this day, with a bottle being auctioned in 2008 and fetching £2,200. So much was salvaged and hidden that some was hidden too well!

Compton Mckenzie wrote *Whisky Galore* after the saga, his vessel called the S.S. Cabinet Minister. It was made into a film, filmed on Barra. Eriskay had had the mother of all binges, putting a new perspective on the old saying 'waiting for my ship to come in'!

Fact File

Getting There

From South Uist by causeway
From Barra by CalMac vehicular ferry
The ferry reaches Eriskay at the side of the beach where Bonnie Prince Charlie landed. The ferry runs daily, check in 10 minutes before departure. Journey time: 40 minutes. There is a causeway from Eriskay to South Uist.

Accommodation

Aird na Haunn, Eriskay, South Uist HS8 5JH
Two 4* self-catering apartments
☎ 0141 339 2143
Bookings to C&A MacDonald, 28 Balshagray Drive, Glasgow, G11 7DD

Kisimul Castle in Castlebay

Barra

The most southerly of the populated islands in the Outer Hebrides is Barra. It claims to be the most beautiful little island in Britain. It is also the only place in Britain where there is a scheduled flight airport, which uses the beach as its runway and where flight times are subject to the state of the tide.

The island consists of hill and moor, stunning sandy beaches and mochair meadowland, a profusion of wild flowers growing on blown sand and blooming at their best in July.

Compton Mackenzie lived here, at Suidheachan, which overlooks Traigh Mhor, the airport's beach. His book, *Whisky Galore*, based on the *S.S. Politician* wreck (see page 28), was made into a film and filmed on Barra. He is buried at Cille Bharra cemetery, Edigarry.

The island was owned by the Chief of the Clan MacNeil, who transferred it (and neighbouring Vatersay) to the Scottish Government in 2003. Today, Barra is home to c. 1,300 people. The main centre of population is Castlebay, where the Oban ferry docks.

A new development in 2008 was the establishment of the Isle of Barra distillery at Borve. All of its first year's production has been reserved, which is an encouraging start. (☎ 01871 8100006, e: sales@barradistillery.co.uk).

Castlebay has the main facilities on the island, including the Post Office, RBS bank, petrol, shops and cafe. The island is approximately 8miles/13km long by 5miles/8km wide and has a ring-road around it. It is fairly hilly, with several reasonably sized hills, the highest being Ben Tangaval in the south west, which rises to 433ft/132m.

Beyond Barra lie the islands of Vatersay, now accessed by a causeway. To the south of here lie Sandray, Pabbay, Mingulay and last in the chain, Berneray, with Barra Head on its south side being the most southern point of the Outer Hebrides. The islands south of Barra have been uninhabited since 1912.

Don't allow yourself to become confused by the multiple use of place names. Barra has four islands called Orosay and there are at least 10 in the Outer Hebrides called either Orosay or Orasay.

Fact File

Getting There

By Sea

CalMac's Oban ferry runs to Castlebay (vehicle check-in 45 minutes, some services are direct and others via Lochboisdale. The direct route takes just under 5 hours) There is an inter-island ferry between Barra and South Uist (Lochboisdale, 1 hour 40 minutes) and also to Eriskay (40 minutes, daily).

By Air

Flybe operates scheduled flights to Barra from Glasgow and Berbecula
☎ 01871 700 0535
www.flybe.com
The Post bus runs from the airport to Castlebay
Barra Terminal info desk: ☎ 01871 890212. There is a cafe at the terminal, at Eoligarry. Terminal closed Sundays.

Accommodation

Hotels

Castlebay Hotel, Castlebay HS9 5XD
☎ 01871 810223
e: info@castlebayhotel.com

Barra

Craigard Hotel, Castlebay HS9 5XD
☎ 01871 810200
e: stay@craigardhotel.co.uk

Heathbank Hotel, Northbay HS9 5YQ
☎ 01871 890266
w: www.barrahotel.co.uk

Isle of Barra Beach Hotel, Tangasdale
☎ 01871 810383
e: barrahotel@aol.com

There are also five B&B's and about 30 self catering holiday homes. The TIC has a booking bureau.

Tourist Information Centre

Main Street, Castlebay HS9 5XD
☎ 01871 810336
Open: Easter-Oct.
(Stornoway TIC, Lewis, is open all year round)

Car Hire

MacMillan Self Drive
☎ 01871 890366

Barra Car Hire
☎ 01871 890313

Taxis
☎ 01871 890253/810999

Bike Hire

(Island Adventurers, see below)
☎ 01871 810284 J. MacDougal

Places to Visit/ Attractions

Barra Heritage Centre
Castlebay HS9 5XD
☎ 01871 810413

Kisimul Castle
On island in the bay,Castlebay. There's a medieval keep and curtain-wall. The castle is in the care of Historic Scotland.
Open: Apr-Sep
☎ 01871 810313
Ticket includes boat out to the castle
w: www.historic-scotland.gov.uk

Vatersay Island
Now joined by a causeway to Barra and situated to the south of the latter.

Macleod's Tower, Loch Tangusdale, A medieval tower house

Golf Course
Grean, Isle of Barra HS9 5XX
☎ 01871 810419
www.isleof barra.com/golf1.html
Nine holes, tickets available from the TIC, Castlebay and at hotels
Most westerly golf course in the UK

Boat trips
Island Adventurers
29 St. Brendan's Rd, Barra HS9 5XJ
Two hour boat trips/charters
☎ 01871 810284

Barra Fishing Charters
Oileag na Mara,
Bruernish, Northbay, HS9 5UY
Also run trips to Mingalay Island, Barra Head and Pabbay, other islands by arrangement
☎ 01871 890384
e: barrafishingchar@aol.com

Sea Kayaking
Clearwater Paddling
Castlebay HS9 5XD
☎ 01871 810443
e: info@ clearwaterpaddling.com

St. Kilda

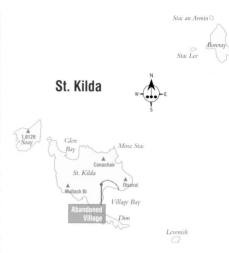

Other than Rockall, St. Kilda is the remotest part of the British Isles and certainly the remotest land mass occupied by people, even if the 'population' is essentially transient. The islands are 41 miles/66km west of Benbecula in the Outer Hebrides.

St. Kilda consists of five main islands – Hirta (the largest island), Soay, Dun, Boraray and Lavanish. The resident population was evacuated in the 1930s. In 1957, St. Kilda was bequeathed to the National Trust for Scotland by the 5th Marquess of Bute and designated a National Nature Reserve. It was Scotland's first World Heritage Site.

On Hirta there is a M.O.D. radar tracking station for its missile range on South Uist.

Management of the islands is now a partnership of the National Trust, Qinetiq (agents for the M.O.D.) and the Western Islands Council. There is a seasonal ranger and an archaeologist

Abandoned Village, St. Kilda

Lamb of the unique Soay breed found on St. Kilda

with conservation and research of the sensitive environment a primary consideration for the National Trust, Scottish Natural Heritage and the M.O.D.

St. Kilda is the most important seabird breeding site in north west Europe. There are huge seabird colonies totalling over 1 million birds, including the world's largest colony of North Atlantic gannets. The Soay sheep plus its field mice and wrens are unique species. The islands were declared to be a UNESCO World Heritage Site in 1986 'for its natural heritage, for its exceptional beauty and for the significant natural habitats it supports'. In July 2004, this was extended to include the surrounding marine environment. This was further extended a year later to Dual World Heritage status for both its natural and cultural significance. St Kilda is the UK's only Dual World Heritage Site.

Visitors are welcome, with a little under 2,000 arrivals per annum. It is however essential that regard for the sensitive environment is maintained.

The Evacuation

The final evacuation of the residents of St. Kilda occurred in 1930. A group had gone earlier and deteriorating circumstances (including an epidemic of wet eczema and crop failure in 1929) made the remaining population realise that maybe life would be better elsewhere. There had been consideration of moving everybody to Canada in 1875, but it seems the majority went for an urban lifestyle in Glasgow and Edinburgh. Some returned in the summertime to renew old memories but a permanent return never presented itself.

The cost of moving the families was c. £800, yet substantial sums were to be spent setting up the M.O.D. base some 25 years later. A pity this injection could not have happened whilst the St. Kildans were still there.

Most of the sheep were rounded up and sold for £800 – there was even a suggestion that it be used to defray the evacuation cost. At 7am on 29th August 1930, the community locked their houses and boarded HMS Harebell and sailed off into history to Oban.

(Evacuation detail based on Francis Thompson's *St. Kilda and Other Hebridean Outliers*, 1988).

Fact File

Getting There

There is no commercial ferry. You therefore arrange your own way of getting there. Join a cruise (if you can) or join a National Trust working party. It is worth contacting the NT for Scotland in the first instance:
Western Isles Manager, National Trust for Scotland, 40 Huntley Street, Inverness IV3 5HR
☎ 01463 232034
There are some rules to be observed. See www.kilda.org.uk/frame2 for the full package of NT for Scotland Advice for Visitors. Boats must land passengers and equipment by dingy to protect the islands from risk of rats or mink getting ashore. Dogs or other pets are not permitted ashore to protect the birds and the Soay sheep.
The St. Kilda Club shop opens for visitors by prior arrangement. On arrival at St. Kilda, contact the St. Kilda Ranger by your vessel's radio – call sign Kilda Warden. The Qinetiq facilities are out of bounds to visitors except in emergency. There is a small museum on the island, its heritage etc. in House 3. The former main street on Hirta still survives with the cottage now roofless, the street now grassed over. It is an evocative sight in a most unusual and awe inspiring destination.
The Scottish Natural Heritage office is at: 135 Stilligarry, South Uist HS8 5RS
☎ 01870 620238 w: www.snh.org.uk

See Uist Outdoor Centre details (p.22) re their ferry service to St. Kilda by RIB (Rigid Inflatable Boat) and Northern Light Charters (p.17).

Rockall

This is the most isolated part of the United Kingdom, being 188miles/301km west of St. Kilda and 287miles/460km from Ardnamurchan Point. It is a vertical sided relatively small lump of rock and difficult to land on or to embark from. It is 63 ft high/19m and 77 ft/23m in diameter at its base. Even in calm weather, there is a significant swell. The *West Coast of Scotland Pilot* advises that 'the islet can best be climbed on its west and north west sides after affecting a landing on a rocky ledge at its south west corner and working along the south west face'. It goes on to add that a landing is only possible after a long period of calm weather, but a heavy swell should be expected.

Interest in the annexation of Rockall was not entirely related to economic reasons (oil and minerals) but to prevent anyone monitoring tests from the rocket firing range on South Uist. Although sovereignty is not disputed, the surrounding continental shelf is subject to claim by the UK, Eire, Denmark and Iceland. Administratively, it is part of the Outer Hebrides.

The Royal Navy put a landing party ashore in 1801 and possession was formally taken by the UK in 1955. In 1985 Tom Maclean (ex-SAS) lived (or rather survived) there for about 6 weeks to press the point of the UK's claim to sovereignty.

Rockall is the name of one of the areas covered by the UK Shipping Forecast. A light was established on the island in 1972 (a red lantern).

The Inner Hebrides

Skye

Skye can be reached across the mainland bridge from Kyle of Lochalsh or by ferry (CalMac) from Mallaig to Armadale. With the Cullin Hills rising dramatically in the south, Skye boasts 13 Munroes (peaks over 3,000ft/914m high). The scenery everywhere is worthy of the visit. Skye really does justify its reputation for grandeur, beauty and enchantment.

Bridge to Isle of Skye

There is much to see and much to do, even if exploring by car rather than with boots or bike. It's worth noting too that despite much holiday accommodation, it all gets booked up in mid and high season, with the population of c. 12,500 rising significantly with the influx of visitors.

Amongst the major attractions are Dunvegan Castle, home of the Clan MacLeod, Armadale Castle, Talisker Distillery and the Aros Centre – great for families and wet weather, near Portree.

Skye is also the ferry terminal (at Uig) for Tarbert on Harris in the Outer Hebrides.

Glenn Heritage, in her guidebook to Skye, tells us that 'Skye is a joy for ramblers and hill walkers with outstanding views at every turn and some of the most dramatic coastal walks in Britain'. For the full story, see her book *Landmark Visitors Guide: Isles of Skye and Raasay*. It gives full information on the island plus tourist services e.g. wildlife tours, details of attractions etc.

The Old Man of Storr
over Loch Leathan

Skye is perhaps best known because of the Skye Boat Song. Flora Macdonald rowed the 'bonnie boat' to Skye and is buried on the island, although she came initially from South Uist, where the remains of her house may be seen. The burial place is near Uig in the cemetery adjacent to the Museum of Island Life.

Fact File

Getting There

Take the spectacular road bridge from Kyle of Lochalsh (Tourist Information Centre ☎ 0800 9804846. This is a private TIC and opens in mid-March) CalMac have a service between Mallaig and Armadale. Check in 30 minutes for vehicles, crossing takes 30 minutes. No winter weekend service nor over Xmas and New Year.

Accommodation

Use the booking agency at Visit Scotland ☎ 0845 22 55 121 or ring one of the Tourist Information Centres on the island (see below).

Tourist Information Centres

Portree ☎ 01478 614906
Dunvegan ☎ 01470 521581
Broadford ☎ 01471 822713

Portree, Isle of Skye

Old Man of Storr, Trotternish Peninsula

Sligachan River

Car Hire

Portree Coachworks
☎ 01476 612688

Ewen MacCree
☎ 01478 612554

Jansvans
☎ 01478 612087

Sutherland Garage
☎ 01471 822225

Taxis

☎ 01470 521560/01478 613456

Cycle Hire

☎ 01470 822270/01478 613121

Places to Visit

Armadale Castle, Gardens and
Museum of the Isles
Armadale IV45 8RS
☎ 01471 844305

Aros Visitor Centre
Viewfield Rd, Portree
☎ 01478 613649

Colbost Croft Museum
4 miles from Dunvegan on Glendale Rd
☎ 10470 521298

Dunvegan Castle
☎ 01470 521206

Glendale Toy Museum
☎ 01470 511240

Isle of Skye Brewery
The Pier, Uig
☎ 01470 542477

Shiasdair
Waternish
☎ 01470 592297
Skye Yarn Co., makers of woollen
sweaters

Skye Serpentarium
The Old Mill
Broadford IV49 9AQ
☎ 01471 822209

Skyeskins
Stein, Waternish
☎ 01470 592237
Tannery with sheepskins etc for sale

Staffin Dinosaur Museum
☎ 01470 562302
Ring in advance

Talisker Distillery
Carbost
☎ 01478 614308

Adventure Sports
Skye Mountain Guides
☎ 01478 612682

Climb Skye
☎ 01478 640264

Skyeadventures
Broadford Pier
☎ 01471 833428

Dive and Sea the Hebrides
Stein, Waternish
☎ 01470 592219

Sea.fari Adventures
Armadale Pier
☎ 01471 833316

Boat Cruises

MV Stardust
☎ 07798 743858

Raasay

Situated between Skye and the mainland is the island of Raasay. Although of comparatively low altitude generally, it does have several hills and Dun Caan rises to 1,465 ft/447m. The island is 14miles/22km in length and up to 5miles/8km in width. There is some forest and much heather clad moorland. The population is c. 200 and most of them live around the village of Inverarish and near to the ferry to Sconsor on Skye.

Inverarish was built to serve a 19th century iron ore mine. A former railway line, which connected the mine with a ferry terminal still exists and it is a short walk to follow it to the mine working, which should not be entered. At Raasay House at Clachan, adjacent Inverarish, there is the Raasay Heritage Centre. It promotes the Gaelic language and the heritage and culture of Raasay.

Nearby is St. Moluag's Chapel, dating from the 11-13th Century. A single road runs up the island northwards and there is a spur, which goes eastwards across the bottom of the island. It passes Brochel Castle, a 14th century fortification belonging to the Macleods. The latter were strong Jacobites and followed Bonnie Prince Charlie. They sheltered the Prince here after Culloden for a couple of nights and paid dearly for their act, with the destruction of their estate here.

With many unspoilt areas and some good walking, Raasay beckons, with the northern end of the island perhaps the best and described in Glen Heritage's book (see below) as "unmissable". There are two deserted villages as a result of the clearances: Umachan and Screapadal. Look out for eagles, sea eagles and red deer.

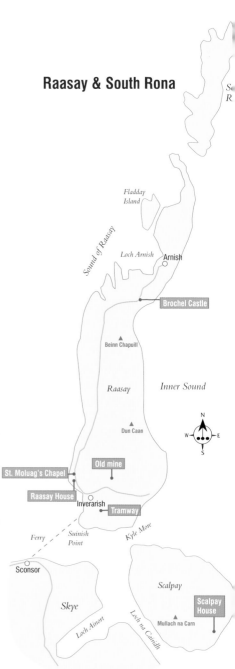

Raasay & South Rona

Fact File

Getting There

CalMac ferry from Sconsor on Skye, takes 25 minutes. Ten minute check-in time. Limited Sunday service. Outside ferry times in summer, a boat from Raasay House will often pick you up from Sconsor. ☎ 01478 660266

Accommodation

Borodale House (was Isle of Raasay Hotel)
Raasay, Isle of Skye IV40 8PB
☎ 01478 660222

Raasay House
Clachan, Raasay
☎ 01478 660266
Offers instruction in sailing, rock climbing, abseiling, kayaking, canoeing and outdoor education. Now operating out of the Borodale House Hotel during the rebuild following a major fire in January 2009

18 Inverarish Cottage
C/o www.highlandholidaycottages.co.uk
☎ 01478 612123

Scottish YHA
Creachan Cottage, Nr. Clachan, Raasay, Isle of Skye IV40 8NT
☎ 08700 041146

South Rona

North of Raasay is the small island of South Rona, with one full time resident who is the agent for the landowner's estate. If you want a holiday really away from it all (well mainly), Rona has three holiday cottages, which have been rebuilt from the ruins of former buildings in what was the hamlet of Dry Harbour. Camping is available plus B&B at the island's only permanent home. For further details contact ronalodge@isleofrona.com or ☎ 07831 293 963.

Reading

Landmark Visitors Guide: Isles of Skye and Raasay by Glenn Heritage £7.99

Rassay Ferry approaching Sconsor on Loch Sligachan

Rum

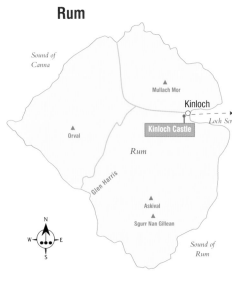

Sound of Canna

Mullach Mor ▲

Kinloch

Orval ▲

Kinloch Castle

Rum

Mallaig/Eigg
Loch Scresort

Glen Harris

Askival ▲

Sgurr Nan Gillean ▲

Sound of Rum

N
W · E
S

Rum

Rum (Rhum) is one of those islands that (at any one time) only had one owner. One of them, Sir George Bullough, left a profound mark, Kinloch Castle, built 1889-1901. The island was purchased by his father in 1888 for £35,000. They were wealthy industrialists who had amassed a fortune from textile machinery.

The huge 'castle' was used as a shooting lodge and as a base to socialise on a grand scale. It was the first private house in Scotland to have electricity. Upon his death in 1957, George bequeathed the place (and island) to the Countryside Commission for Scotland. Since 1992 it has been vested in Scottish Natural Heritage, the island being declared a National Nature Reserve in c. 1957.

The house continued in the occupation of Lady Monica Bullough until her death, but it remained an Edwardian time-warp. It is open daily (but not Sundays) and one hour tours coincide with the ferry's arrival. It is

slowly decaying for want of restoration and although featured on BBC's *Restoration* programme in 2003, it failed to win and attract the £3m prize. The Friends of Kinloch Castle Association welcomes members as it tries to steer restoration to this unique building and contents.

Rum is 8.5miles/13.5km by 8miles/13km in extent. Several peaks are over 2,000ft/610m high, the highest being at Haskeval at 2,667ft/813m. At the beginning of the 20th century, the population was 149. It now has a permanent population c. 25 people.

The island has a community shop/post office next to the village hall, run by volunteers. It opens 5-7.30pm (and may be open during the day). There is a craft shop co-operative open most afternoons selling local products. The teashop in the community hall opens daily from 11am- 4pm between April and September.

In 2008, the Scottish Government announced the decision to set up to five crofts and the 'development of a dynamic community on Rum, which is not solely dependent on Scottish Natural Heritage'.

The island has some 200 archaeological sites and monuments.

Wildlife

There are 61,000 Manx Shearwaters here (1/3rd world population); red deer, 3-4 pairs of golden eagles and white tailed sea eagles. The latter have been steadily reintroduced to Scotland starting here and now there are in the region of three dozen in the Western Isles. Worms on Rum are the largest in the UK and there are over 400 feral goats. You are likely to see the Rum pony; it is smaller than the Highland and the Skye ponies. There is a wildlife exhibition in the boat shed by the old pier.

Midges are pretty bad here; a head net is

available in the community shop. Access to Kilmory and Kilmory Glen may be restricted in mid-September to Mid-November when the deer are rutting.

Rum National Reserve
Reserve Office, Rum PH43 4RR
☎ 01687 462026

Fact File

Getting There

Cars are not permitted, but dogs are welcome if on a lead. Vehicles are only carried with a previously obtained permit (available only to bone fide tradesmen or those with a disability permit. The CalMac timetable gives phone numbers for the relevant island). CalMac ferries from Mallaig either direct to Rum or via Eigg (summer service). The direct route takes 1 hour 20 minutes. Foot passengers last check-in 15 minutes before sailing. (30 minutes for vehicles or if excess baggage)
☎ 01687 462403

Shearwater Cruises, Arisaig ☎ 01687 450224 W: www.arisaig.co.uk; e: info@ arisaig.co.uk
Cruises to Rum, Eigg and Muck from Arisaig.

Accommodation

There is a hostel at the rear of Kinloch Castle (self catering or full board). It has a bar, open to non-residents.
☎ 01687 462037
e: kinlochcastle@snh.gov.uk

Camping

There is a limited facility campsite near the shoreline. Wild camping is permitted, but notify the SNH Ranger beforehand. Fires are not permitted; avoid disturbing the wildlife (the island is a National Nature Reserve).
☎ 01687 462026
There are also two bothies run by the Mountain Bothies Association at Dibidil in the south and Guirdil in the west.

Eigg

Situated 7.5miles/12km west of Arisaig, the island is approximately 6.25miles/10km long and 4 miles/6km wide. At the southern end, a promontory rises to a peak 1,289ft/393m high and called the Scuir of Eigg. The sound between Eigg and Castle Island in the south gives shelter to vessels.

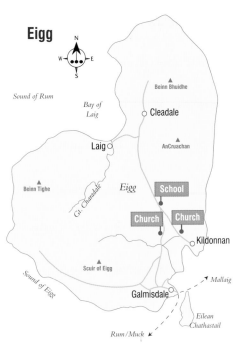

Laig Bay & the crofting township of Cleadale

Eigg has the Small Isles parish church; The Lodge and its exotic gardens were constructed in the 1920s by Lord Runciman, the President of the Board of Trade. It is the only substantial dwelling on the island. On the 12th June 1997, the island was purchased by the islanders, who established the Eigg Heritage Trust. The Trust has built the An Laimtirig Centre which houses the Eigg Shop and Post Office ☎ 01687 482432 (e: sue.kirk@btopenworld.com); the Tea Room, which doubles up as the bar/restaurant in the evenings; the Craft Shop run by an island co-operative; and the toilets/shower.

Like most of the neighbouring islands, the bird population draws the enthusiasts. In an average year some 130 species are recorded. The island has a Scottish Wildlife Trust warden

Laig Bay looking over to Rum

☎ 01687 482477. (www.swt.org.uk). The island website lists details of ceilidhs and other events on the island. (www.isleofeigg.org)

Fact File

Getting There

CalMac ferries run from Mallaig to Eigg. There are also boats to Eigg from Rum and Muck but these services are not daily and you should check details with the ferry company ☎ 01687 462403. Vehicles are only carried with a previously obtained permit (available only to bone fide tradesmen or those with a disability permit. The CalMac timetable gives phone numbers for the relevant island).

Accommodation

Bed & Breakfast

Lageorna ☎ 01687 482405
e: sue@lageorna.com

Kildonan House ☎ 01687 482446

Self Catering

Glebe Barn 4* ☎ 01687 482417
e: simon@glebebarn.co.uk

Top House e: scwmartins@hotmail.com

Glebe Cottage ☎ 01687 482422
e: glebecot@hotmailcom

Cuagach Bothy ☎ 01687 482486
e: maggie@isleofeigg.net

Clanranald Cottage ☎ 01687 462874

Sandavore Farmhouse
☎ 01687 482438
up to 8 and cottage for 2+2

Muck

Muck

The smallest of the four Small Isles group (with Rum, Eigg and Canna in descending order of size). It covers 1,586acres/709hec and is approximately 2miles/3km long and 1mile/1.6km in width. Its population is small too c. 38 people. The harbour is at Port Mor and the only road runs 1.5miles/2.4km to the only farm on the island at Gallanach. Vehicles can be driven ashore up a slipway, but as they are not usually permitted it offers little advantage. The farm carries cattle and sheep and offers private charter on a motor launch. Ring ☎ 01687 462362 for details.

There is a craft shop selling local produce, including Isle of Muck lamb plus a tearoom near the pier. There are walks up Beinn Airen (449ft/137m) and to Horse Island at low tide to view the bird life. Alternatively, bikes may be hired at the craft shop. The diving is good here and Muck has the only British Coral (the Cup Coral). The grey seal is a common sight and clearly likes the warm seas of the area.

Fact File

Getting There

CalMac operate a ferry from Mallaig, 2.25 hours away. The latest check-in time is 15 minutes prior to sailing (longer if you have excess baggage). Vehicles are only carried with a previously obtained permit (available only to bone fide tradesmen or those with a disability permit. The CalMac timetable gives phone numbers for the relevant island). The ferries run 3 days a week (not on Mon, Wed). You can see most of the four islands on a day cruise, plus accompanying whales, dolphins and porpoises. There are other day cruises from both Mallaig and Arisaig. Arisaig Marine offer cruises which allow 2-5 hours ashore on the various islands. It leaves Arisaig at 11.00am and returns 5-6pm. Their ferry runs four times a week (Mon, Wed, Fri and Sun).
☎ 01687 450224
☎ 01687 450678
w: www.arisaig.co.uk

Accommodation

Port Mor House Hotel
☎ 01687 462365
e: hotel@isleofmuck.com
Only hotel on the island

Bed and Breakfast

Carn Dearg
☎ 01687 462363
e: carndearg@yahoo.co.uk

Godag House
☎ 01687 462371

Holiday Cottages (3)
☎ 01687 462362
e: info@isleofmuck.com

Bunkhouse
☎ 01687 462042

Craft Shop and Tea Room
☎ 01687 462362
Local lamb delivered from here to Mallaig or Arisaig for collection

Events

Muck has an open day in June. Contact Arisaig Maritime to book the ferry (see above).

Canna

Canna is the most westerly of the four islands known as Small Islands – Rum, Eigg and Muck being the other three. It is situated to the north west of Rum and consists of Canna and Sanday Islands. The former is about 5 miles/8km long by 1.25m/2km wide. Sanday is smaller, 1 mile long/1.6km x 0.25m wide and is joined to Canna by a road bridge superseding a link road which used to flood at high tide.

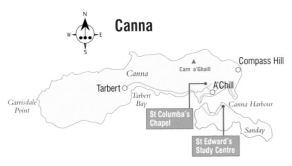

Canna

Canna is 2,700 acres/1093hec in extent and rises up to 689ft/210m at Carn a' Ghaill hill. There are a few working crofts and a population of 12, including two families who were successful in applying to an offer to go and live there in 2006.

The islands were left to the National Trust for Scotland (NTS) by J L Campbell in 1981, subject to his widow's occupation of Canna House where she (American musician Margaret Fay Shaw) resided until her death in 2004. There are two large houses, Canna House and Tighard. Canna House has J L Campbell's important archive of Gaelic interest. A tea room and a post office have been built plus a toilet/shower for campers, but no shop. You either take it with you or phone the Spar shop in Mallaig and they will send your groceries over to the island. Whilst there is a phone connection, there is no mobile phone coverage available.

The pier has been rebuilt and enlarged, but only residents' cars are permitted to land. Canna Habour is a deep-water natural harbour sheltered by two islands and is a popular anchorage for yachts. It is the only deep harbour anchorage in the Small Isles. However, the iron-rich volcanic rock of Compass Hill plays havoc with a ship's compass!

The islands are a haven for bird life (as one might expect). There is also a species of wood mice of Viking provenance and these were removed (at least some of them) prior to the extermination of the resident rat population (estimated at 10,000). The mice were then reintroduced and seem to be doing well along with Manx Shearwaters, puffins and razorbills. The island has been a bird sanctuary since 1938 and some 160 species are recorded annually. The coastline is a Special Protection Area.

Fact File

Getting There

CalMac run a ferry to Canna from Mallaig via Rum. The time is 55 minutes from Rum and 1 hour 20 minutes from Mallaig to Rum. There is also a ferry direct from Muck to Canna (1 hour 35 minutes). Vehicles are only carried with a previously obtained permit (available only to bone fide tradesmen or those with a disability permit. The CalMac timetable gives phone numbers for the relevant island).

Accommodation

The NTS has self-catering accommodation for 4 people at Lag nam Boitean, plus The Bothy which sleeps 2. Contact the NTS holiday team ☎ 0844 4932108; e: holidays@nts.org. uk.

B&B
Tighard Guest House
☎ 01687 462474.

Wild camping is permitted.

On Sanday the former St. Edward's Chapel and Point House is now the St. Edward's Study Centre, opened by the Princess Royal in 2001. It offers accommodation for up to 12 people and is run by the Hebridean Trust (North Parade Chambers, 75a Banbury Rd., Oxford OX2 6PE ☎ 01865 311468).

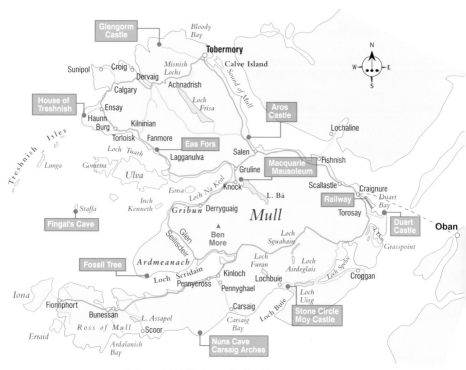

Isles of Mull, Iona & Staffa

Mull

Mull has long been popular with visitors. Dr Johnson and his biographer, James Boswell, came here in 1773 on their tour of the Highlands. Today it has gained popularity through the TV series Balamory which was filmed in Tobermory, the different painted harbour-side buildings being well recognised by many prospective visitors. For many visitors the approach from Oban is all the more impressive with the view to Duart Castle, perched upon a bluff at the entrance to the Sound of Mull. It is passed shortly before the ferry boat docks at neighbouring Craignure.

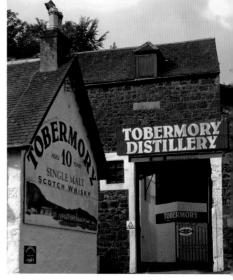

Tobermory Distillery, on the quay at Tobermory

Loch Scridain

Duart Castle

Visitors from Mallaig or Fort William can take a quicker route by using the short Lochaline to Fishnish ferry, also across the Sound of Mull or the Kilchoan – Tobermory crossing, which offers the advantage of a trip along the scenic coastline of Loch Sunart to Kilchoan on Ardnamurchan.

Well known for its lovely scenery, Mull lends itself to a couple of easy scenic routes, although both can be achieved in a day if your time is short. From Tobermory (the town has the usual town services) go west on the B8073 to Dervaig, with its unusual church tower and on to Calgary with its large beach. The road heads south west, down the side of Loch Tuath, with views out to Ulva and Gometra Islands. It climbs a little before dropping down to Loch Na Keal.

At the head of the loch the B8035 may be taken to the left to Salen and the A848 back to Tobermory along the Sound of Mull. Alternatively, the B8035 to the right (at Gruline) hugs the coast along Loch Na Keal's south east side skirting Ben More, the island's highest mountain at 3,169ft/966m. The road climbs away from the loch before descending to Loch Scridain. At the A849 you can go left, back to the Sound of Mull via Craignure, with the opportunity of visiting Duart Castle, the home of Chief of the Clan Maclean, or Torosay Castle with its 12acre/5ha gardens. If you choose to go right on the A849, the road leads to the peninsula of the Ross of Mull and the villages of Bunessan and Fionnphort, where the ferry crosses over to nearby Iona. There is some impressive scenery to be seen touring Mull with many memorable views.

Tobermory

Calgary Bay

Fact File

Getting There

CalMac ferries: Oban – Craignure;
Lochaline – Fishnish; Kilchoan
– Tobermory (ferry not bookable).

Laga Bay, Ardnamurchan to Tobermory
Book at least one day in advance, runs
Monday and Friday
Also Tobermory and Drimnin (on
Morvern), also runs Monday and Friday
Ardcharters
☎ 01972 500208
e: ardcharters@aol.com
The ferry runs from Laga to Tobermory
in early morning, plies between
Tobermory and Drimnin (one trip
each way) in the morning and again
in the afternoon before returning from
Tobermory to Laga; winter timetable
slightly different. Foot passengers only,
ferry not bookable. The same company
offers self-catering accommodation
on the small Isle of Carna, opposite
Laga, in Loch Sunart. A 16ft/5m boat
is included and the house sleeps 6
people.

Accommodation

Contact the Tourist Information Centre
at Craignure
☎ 08707 200610/08452 255121
e: info@mull.visitscotland.com
Also at Tobermory (April – October)
☎ 08707 200625/08452 255121

Boat Trips/Wildlife Tours

Ardnamurchan Charters
(see above)

Wildlife Expectations
Ulva Ferry
☎ 01688 500121
w: www.scotlandlife.com

Explore Mull Wildlife
Dervaig
☎ 01688 400209

M.V. Volante
Fionnphort/Iona
☎ 01681 700362
w: www.volanteiona.com

There are a lot more than these. The Tourist Information Centre can give more details.

Car Hire

Craignure ☎ 01680 812444
Tobermory ☎ 01688 302103

Cycle Hire

Craignure ☎ 01680 812496
Tobermory ☎ 01688 302020

Pony Trekking

Killiechronan ☎ 0774 8807 447

Places to Visit

An Tobar
Tobermory PA 75 6PB
☎ 01688 302211
Arts Centre and Gallery

Burg National Scenic Area
Tiroran
☎ 01463 232034
North side of Loch Scridain. Open daily

Duart Castle, Craignure
☎ 01680 812309

Narrow Gauge Railway
☎ 01680 812494

Tobermory Distillery
☎ 01688 302647

Tobermory Museum
☎ 01688 302493

Torosay Castle, Craignure
☎ 01680 812470

Iona

Situated off the south west tip of Mull is the island of Iona. Only 3.5m/6km in length and about 1 mile/2km in width, it is believed to be the earliest Christian settlement in Scotland. Today the abbey is a source of pilgrimage, although having to pay an entrance fee may be considered a bit much at such a holy site.

The ferry from Fionnphort has frequent sailings bringing in visitors disgorging from buses. Most of them walk from the ferry to the abbey church and back. Others come here for periods of quiet contemplation, although 'quiet' must be denied them in the busy area during the day. Elsewhere, the rest of the island must be ideal.

Having left the ship the main street runs inland passed a long row of houses, which makes up the most of the community in the village. Continue inland a short distance up the street with its few shops to where a right turn for the abbey leads past the Nunnery, now a ruin. It dates from 1200 AD and the area is now a garden. The path leads on to the island school, a few more shops and the parish church, with the Abbey complex ahead.

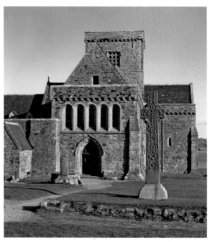

Iona Abbey

Iona from the quay side

The Nunnery, Iona

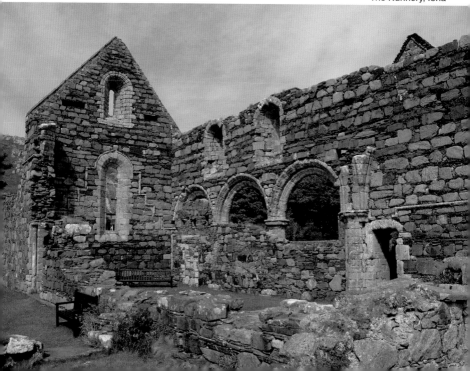

Ancient cross, Iona

The abbey is approached through a burial ground, which contains the remains of 48 Scottish kings, including Macbeth. Look out for the grave of John Smith too, the Labour Party Leader, who died in 1994. Nearby is St. Oran's Chapel where quiet contemplation may be more of a possibility than in the abbey church itself.

At the beginning of the 20th Century, the abbey church was placed by the Duke of Argyll into the hands of the Iona Cathedral Trust and its restoration commenced. The abbey dates from 1203. Perhaps it is worth considering an early morning visit if you savour visiting such a prestigious place under conditions where some better degree of reverence is possible.

Fact File

Getting There

CalMac ferry from Fionnphort. Frequent sailings during the daytime. See below for evening ferry details after CalMac finish (6.15pm from Iona between end of March and late October summer timetable). Sailing time: 10 minutes, check-in time is 10 minutes.

Bus services to Fionnphort ☎ 0871 200 2233. CalMac advise that passengers for the 1520 bus Fionnphort – Craignure (Mon-Fri) should depart Iona no later than 14.45.

Accommodation

Argyll Hotel
Isle of Iona, Argyll PA76 6SJ
☎ 01681 700334
e: reception@argyllhoteliona.co.uk

St. Columba Hotel
PA76 6SL
☎ 01681 700304
e: info@stcolumbahotel.co.uk

Retreat Breaks

Bishop's House, Iona PA76 6SJ
Retreat Centre for groups and individuals
☎ 01681 700800

Cnoc a'Chalmain, Iona PA76 6SP
Roman Catholic House of Prayer
☎ 01681 700369

Duncraig, Iona PA76 6SP
Ideal for singles/small groups
☎ 01681 700202

Other Facilities

Taxi
☎ 01681 700776/0781 032 5990

Bike Hire
☎ 01681 700357/700365

Spar Shop
☎ 01681 700321

Places to Visit

Iona Abbey & Nunnery
Isle of Iona, Argyl
☎ 01681 700512
Open: daily at all times

Iona Heritage Centre
Iona PA76 6SJ
☎ 01681 700328
Open: Apr-Oct, Mon-Sat, 2.30-4.30pm

Columba Steadings Arts & Crafts
Iona PA76 6SW
☎ 01681 700121
Open: daily, Apr-Oct

Finlay, Ross Ltd
Martyr's Bay PA76 6SP
☎ 01681 700357
Outdoor clothing, Celtic jewellery,

crafts, cycle hire, B&B
Open: daily Apr-Oct, 9.30am-6pm; Nov-Mar, Mon-Sat 10am-3.30pm

Iona Gallery & Pottery
Iona PA76 6SW
☎ 01681 700439
Open: Apr-Sep, 11am-4pm
(approximately)

Aosdana Gallery
Aosdana, The Columba Steadings,
Iona PA76 6SW
☎ 01681 700121

Iona Tapestries
☎ 01681 700335

Iona One Arts & Crafts
☎ 01681 700001

Oran Creative Crafts
☎ 01681 700127

Boat Trips

Alternative Boat Hire
Mark Jardine, Lovedale, Iona PA76 6SJ
☎ 01681 700537
Inshore trips in traditional wooden open boat

Staffa Boat Trips
Tigh na Traigh PA76 6SJ
☎ 01681 700358

MV Volante
Whale watching/wildlife trips
☎ 01681 700362
w: www.volanteiona.com
Also sea angling trips and evening ferry services (after CalMac have finished for the day) from Iona to Fionnphort

Further Reading

Landmark Visitors Guide: Mull, Iona & Staffa, H.M. Peel £7.99

Ulva & Gometra

Ulva

The Isle of Ulva lies off the west coast of Mull. It is 5m/8km long and up to nearly 2.5m/4km wide. It has a population of c. 26 and is privately owned. Access is only one minute across the water and there are no tarmac-sealed roads, so cars are not allowed. The population are engaged in cattle and sheep farming, fish and oyster farming plus tourism. It is worth including the island on your Mull itinerary. Just turn up at Ulva Ferry and ring the bell for the ferryman. The ferry is open Mon-Fri 9am-5pm, also Sun June–Aug (not open Sat). Bikes permitted. Camping is permitted, ring in advance to book. (☎ 01688 500264 or e: ulva@mull.com)

Ulva from Ulva Ferry

There are several walking trails varying from one to five hours in length. The wildlife is varied and if you are lucky you may see otters, red deer, eagles and the illusive corncrake. The island is partly wooded and reaches a height of 1,019 ft/3l0m. Dr. Johnson and his biographer, James Boswell, visited Ulva to see its basaltic columns and there are more on Gometra adjacent. Ulva is owned by the Howard family of Ulva House.

Gometra

This small island is just off the west end of Ulva, it reaches a height of 497 ft/151m and has a lot of columnar basalt, but is less well known for this than Staffa, which is much smaller and to the south west. Gometra is connected to Ulva by a small causeway at the northern end, which permits access at low tide.

Treshnish Isles

Unpopulated and situated west of Ulva.

Fact File

Getting There
Cruises from Ulva Ferry, Mull and Oban

Turus Mara
Penmore Mill, Dervaig, Mull PA75 6QS
☎ 01688 400242
e: info@turusmara.com
Wildlife and Seabird Cruises, trips also to Staffa and Iona

From Fionnphort
Gordon Grant Marine
Archavaich, Iona
☎ 01681 700338

Places to Visit

Heritage Centre
Isle of Ulva, Ulva Ferry, Isle of Mull
☎ 01688 500241/500266
e: ulva@mull.com

The Boathouse
Licensed Tea Room
Tea to three course meals available
☎ 01688 500241

Sheila's Cottage
Reconstructed traditional thatched croft-house, now a museum.

Also from Oban

Staffa

Staffa is well known as being the site of Fingal's Cave, perhaps the best known sea-cave in Britain. Uninhabited since at least Victorian times, Staffa lies 6 miles/9.5km north of Iona and the same distance from the nearest point of Mull. It is 54 miles/87km west of Oban. It is about 1.5 miles/2km in circumference and rises to a height of just under 150 ft/46m. It is famous for its six-sided columnar basalt formations, similar to those at the Giants Causeway in N. Ireland.

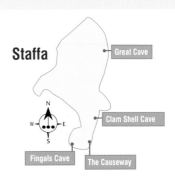

Staffa

- Great Cave
- Clam Shell Cave
- Fingals Cave
- The Causeway

Fingal's Cave is the largest of several caverns, which pierce the basalt rock. It is 227 ft/69m long, 42 ft/13m wide and about 60 ft/18m high. There is a stairway up onto the flat top of the cliffs at Clamshell Cave and a 300yd/274m causeway to Fingal's Cave along the tops of the basalt columns, similar to Giants Causeway, from where the boat docks.

Hilary Peel, in her *Landmark Visitor's Guide Mull, Iona & Staffa* describes the view back to the cave entrance from a boat inside the cave: "Iona floats on the serenely shining sea. The solemnity, reminiscent of a cathedral, induces a meditative mood as the water sighs and susarates, breathing gently and deeply around you". To experience this for yourself, see details below. Note that there are no facilities ashore.

This island is now owned by the National Trust for Scotland (☎ 01463 232034) and was declared a National Nature Reserve in 2001. It has a large seabird population, with dolphins, porpoises and sometimes a whale to be observed in the surrounding sea. The island is fertile and once supported a couple of crofts.

Staffa is open daily but boat tours tend to be seasonal.

Fact File

Getting There

To Staffa and Treshnish Isles

Ardnamurchan Charters

Glenborrowdale
☎ 01972 500208
e: ardcharters@aol.com

From Mull

Craignure
☎ 01680 812377; Tobermory
☎ 01688 302182

Turus Mara

Penmore Mill, Dervaig, Mull PA75 6QS
☎ 01688 400242
e: info@turusmara.com
Wildlife and Seabird Cruises

From Iona

C. Kirkpatrick, Tigh na Traigh (☎ 01681 700358; e: iolare@staffatrips.co.uk)
Offer a three hour trip with at least one hour ashore.

Gordon Grant Tours

☎ 01681 700338

Above: Fingal's Cave

Opposite: Basalt rock columns and cliff face, Staffa

Coll

Similar to nearby Tiree, Coll has numerous white sandy beaches and a high sunshine record. It also claims that its main attraction is that it has no attractions. Also like Tiree, it has a hill Ben Hogh at 341 ft/104m. It does have a RSPB reserve, so one supposes the marketing strap line of 'no attractions' isn't quite true. What it endeavours to emphasise is that the attraction is its natural attractions.

It has been attracting visitors to see them for some time too. Dr. Johnson and his biographer, James Boswell, were stranded here in the 18th century for ten days because of a storm. Then the island supported a good population centred on farming and fishing. It is now just c. 150 people.

The island is 13 miles/21km long and about 3 miles/5km wide, similar in fact to neighbouring Tiree. It has a couple of castles, the oldest being the 15th century Breachachamed Castle, with a square keep, restored a few years ago. The other was built in 1750 for Hector Maclean. At Killunaig are the remains of a medieval church, which no doubt catered for the spiritual needs of a long vanished larger population.

The children's books by Kate Morage are set on Coll, which is the Isle of Struay in her books.

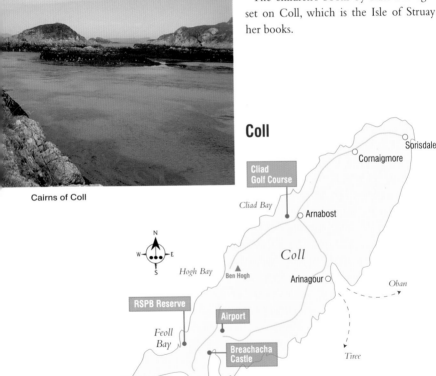

Cairns of Coll

Fact File

Getting There

CalMac operates a service to Coll from Oban but not Wed and Fri (summer service). The ferry goes to Arinagour on Coll. It takes 2 hours 40 (or 55) minutes. There is also a service from Tiree to Oban via Coll, daily except Tues.

Highland Airways operate from Oban to Tiree and Coll and British Airways fly to Tiree, necessitating a ferry trip to Coll (one hour away) subject to availability.

Accommodation

Coll Hotel
Isle of Coll, Argyll PA78 6SZ
☎ 01879 230334
e: info@collhotel.com
Winner: The Scottish Hotel of the Year Award

Places to Visit

Well, it is not quite 'no attractions'. The RSPB reserve offers guided tours in summer and there are guided tours of the island by the Argyll Islands Tourist Guides Association, operated by the Ross of Mull Heritage Centre ☎ 01681 700656.

The Arinagour shop and post office also has bikes for hire ☎ 01879 230395.

Island Stores, Arinagour PA78 6SY
☎ 01879 230484

Taxi

☎ 01879 230402

Golf

There is a nine-hole golf course.

Tiree

Tiree is the flattest of all the Inner Hebridean islands with most of it being lower than 50 ft/15m, although Beinn Hynish rises up to just below 450 ft/137m. With a coastline of 46 miles/74km, length of 10 miles/16km and width of 3 miles/5km, it is also one of the larger islands. It is in fact the 20th largest around Britain.

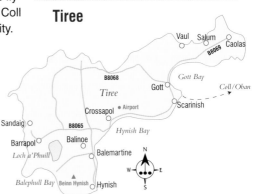

Tiree

Situated 2 miles/3km west of the Ardnamurchan peninsula, it is noted for its white shell-sand beaches, with Gott Bay being 2.5 miles/4km in length. It is a windy island, which has the effect of driving the midges away. It is also under the influence of the Gulf Stream, with some of the highest levels of sunshine recorded in Britain. The island is also noted for its spring time profusion of flowers, but absent of any woodland. Some of its birdlife is special too, with varieties such as the corncrake surviving in the machair grassland.

Like many of the Scottish islands, there is evidence of occupation going back to towards prehistory. There are over twenty Iron Age forts and 2 brochs.

Columbus founded here a daughter monastery of the abbey at Iona, where he had settled in 563 AD.

Bales of Hay, Tiree

Fact File

Getting There

Tiree Airport
☎ 01879 220456 Info: ☎ 01879 220309
w: www.hial.co.uk

Flights with Flybe ☎ 0871 700 0535

Highland Airways ☎ 0845 450 2245

CalMac operates a ferry from Oban on the Coll/Tiree route. It takes 3hrs 40mins to 4 hours 5 mins and is currently experimenting with a Road Equivalent Tariff where the fare is on a mileage basis. The ferry runs daily in summer, usually with an early start. Latest check-in time, 30 minutes for vehicles except Oban, 45 minutes.

Car Hire

Maclennans ☎ 01879 220555
Tiree Motor Co ☎ 01879 220469

Argyll & Bute Council provides an 'on demand dial a bus' transport service.
☎ 01879 220419 to book.
Argyll & Island Tourist Board
☎ 01631 563122

Accommodation

Scarinish Hotel
Scarinish, Isle of Tiree PA77 6UH
☎ 01879 220308
e: info@tireescarinishhotel.com

For other accommodation see www.isleoftiree.com/accommodation.

Campsite

Balinoe, Burnside Cottage, Cornaig PA77 6XA
☎ 07712 159205

Wild Diamond Watersports
Details as campsite above
Wind and kite surfing, sand-yachting plus other adventure sports.

Events

Tiree is home to the **Tiree Wave Classic**. This is a world championship windsurfing event held in October. **Bumblebee World**, held at the end of June, celebrates the fact that the island is home to three of the rarest bumblebees in the UK, including the only Scottish location for the red-shanked Carder bee.

Places to Visit

Sandaig Island Life Museum
A terrace of ancient, thatched buildings restored in 1992 by the Hebridean Trust. The Trust has also restored the Hynish Museum, which also offers group accommodation.
☎ 01879 220726
e: info@hebrideantrust.org

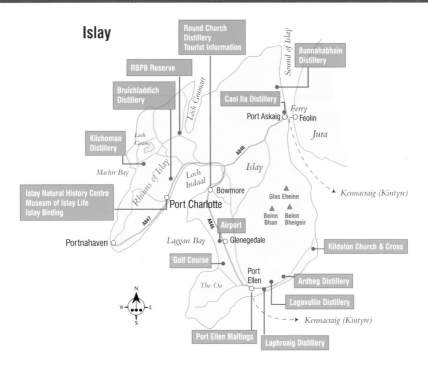

Islay

This lovely island lies at the entrance to the Firth of Lorne. It is home to 3,200 people and there is much to see and do here, let alone seeking out its local produce, such as Spirited Soaps of Bowmore, with its 'soap scented with famous whisky'. It has stunning beaches, great wildlife, especially the birds, with a large winter population of geese and numerous corncrake and chough, now so rare on much of the mainland.

The craggy coastline of the Mull Of Oa, Islay

Islay

Portnahavn, picturesque fishing village in the southwest of Islay. Lighthouse offshore on a small isle

Islay is also famous for its malt whisky, with no less than eight distilleries on the island and yet another former distillery, the Port Ellen Maltings, which now provides malt for the production process. Details of tours of the distilleries are given below.

The island is a mix of good farmland and lochan-studdied moorland. It is proud of its Kildalton Cross, well worth going to see on the minor road up the coast from Port Ellen. It is about 8 ft/2m in height and is the last unbroken ringed Celtic cross in Scotland, dating from c. 800 AD.

The best of the beaches face the Atlantic and are to be found at Machir Bay, Saligo Bay and at Sanaigmore. The island is characterised by small villages and single-storey cottages, snug up against the coast and with some interesting places to see, such as the round church at Bowmore.

Islay is well known for its Festival of Malt & Music held in May. The musical theme continues with a Chamber Music Festival during the summer and a jazz festival in September. There is a book festival also in September and a half marathon in August.

oystercatcher (haematopus ostralegus), shy and frequent resident of the coastlands

Carraig Fhada lighthouse, Islay

Red deer on Jura

Fact File

Getting There

CalMac from Kennacraig to Port Ellen and Port Askaig. Check-in Kennacraig 30 minutes, others 45 minutes for vehicles.

Daily sailings in summer. Timetable subject to alteration at short notice. It is 2 hours 20 minutes to Port Ellen and 2 hours 5 minutes to Port Askaig.

There is a small airport in the south of the island, close to Laggan Bay at Glenegedale, PA42 7AS).
☎ 01496 30236
Scheduled service from Glasgow (Flybe) ☎ 0871 700 0535
Terminal open: 8.30am-6.00pm (Mon-Fri); to 10am on Saturday and on Sunday from 4-6pm.
Bicycle hire at airport.

Accommodation

Contact Tourist Information (see below).

Car Hire

Mackenzies ☎ 01496 302300
Islay Car Hire ☎ 01496 810544

Taxis

☎ 01496 302155/302622/810449

Distillery Information

Ardbeg Distillery
☎ 01496 302244
w: www.ardbeg.com
Open: Mon-Fri, tour times 10.30am & 3pm in winter; from Easter-August open daily, tour times 10.30am, 12noon and 3pm.
Founded 1815

Above and below: Ardbeg Distillery

Bowmore Distillery
☎ 01496 810671
w: www.bowmore.distillery@ morrisonbowmore.com
Open: Easter-Jun, Mon-Sat 9am-5pm, tours 10am, 11am, 2pm, 3pm;
Jul-mid-Sep, Mon-Sun 9am-5pm, tours 10am, 11am, 2pm, 3pm
Other periods: Mon-Fri 9am-5pm, tours 10am, 11am, 2pm, 3pm; Sat 9-noon, tour 10am.
No charge under 18s
Founded 1779
Bowmore has its own cottage accommodation.

Bruichladdich Distillery
Bruichladdich PA49 7UN
☎ 01496 850190
w: www.bruichladdich.com
Please book your visit
Tours mary@bruichladdich.com
Open: Easter-Sep, Mon-Fri 9am-5pm; Sat 10am-4pm, tours 10.30am, 11.30am, 2.30pm; Sat 10.30am & 2.30pm. Oct-Easter, tours Mon-Fri 11.30am & 2.30pm; Sat 11.30am
Founded 1881

Bunnahabhain Distillery
Post Askraig, Islay PA46 7RP
☎ 01496 840646
w: www.bunnahabhain.com
Open: mid-Apr to mid-Oct, Mon-Fri, tours 10.30am, 2pm & 3.15pm. Rest of year by appointment only
Founded 1882

Caol Ila Distillery
Port Askaig PA46 7RL
☎ 01496 302760
w: www.caolila.distillery@diageo.com
Open: Mon-Fri by appointment all year
Founded 1846

Kilchoman Distillery
Rockside Farm, Bruichladdich PA49 7UT
☎ 01496 850011
Open: Apr-Oct, Mon-Sat, 10am-5pm, tours at 11am and 3pm.
Winter: Mon-Fri, times as above
Opened 2005, first distillery on the island in 124 years. Café and shop

Lagavulin Distillery
Port Ellen PA42 7DZ
☎ 01496 302400
Open all year, tours by appointment, Monday - Friday

Laphroaig Distillery
Port Ellen PA42 7DU
☎ 01496 302418
w: www.laphroaig.com
Open: Mon-Fri, 10.15am & 2.15pm. Please book. Distillery usually closed for maintenance in July & August every year.
Founded pre-1818

Port Ellen Maltings
Former distillery, only open by arrangement or at the annual Islay Malt Whisky Festival

Places to Visit

Islay Natural History Centre
Port Charlotte PA48 7TX
☎ 01496 850288
Open: Jun-Aug, Mon-Sat 10am-4pm; Apr, May, Sep, Oct, open Mon-Friday
Ideal for a rainy day, in same buildings as the youth hostel

Museum of Islay Life
Port Charlotte PA48 7UA
☎ 01496 850358
w: www.islaymuseum.org

RSPB Nature Reserve
Bushmills Cottage PA44 7PR
☎ 01496 850505
Visitor centre open daily 10am-5pm
Head of Loch Gruinort, stunning views, unusually includes working farm.
Extends to 4000 ac/1600ha.

RSPB Nature Reserve
The Oa
Situated in the far south. Open at all times and free entrance. Consists of rugged coast and moorland. Two guided walks from May-Sep

One of 2 round churches in the UK at Bowmore, Islay (the other is at Cambridge)

Spirited Soaps
Bowmore ☎ 01496 810938

Activities

Pony Trekking
Ballivicar Farm, Port Ellen PA42 7AW
☎ 01496 302251
w: www.ballivicar.co.uk
Also 3 s.c. apartments; pony trekking and carriage riding

Island Tours
Lady of the Isles
39 Stanalane, Bowmore PA43 7LA
☎ 07732 283554/01496 810485
Minibus, seats 7

Islay Birding
Old Byre, Main Street, Port Charlotte PA48 7TX
☎ 01496 850010
e: info@islaybirding.co.uk

Tourist Information Centre
The Square, Bowmore PA43 7JP
☎ 01496 810254/08707 200617

e: islay@visitscotland.com
For accommodation and general enquiries

Machrie Golf Course/Hotel, Port Ellen
☎ 01496 302310
18 holes, near the airport

Islay Hospital ☎ 01496 301000

Jura

Jura is one of the larger islands, being fourth largest in the Inner Hebrides. It is c. 28 miles/40km long plus 7-8 miles/12km in wide. It covers 142 sq miles and has three mountains in the south. The Paps of Jura are too low for Munroe status but the highest still reach a credible height of 2,575 ft/785m.

Malt whisky drinkers will have heard of this island. Isle of Jura malt has been made since 1810. Produced by Whyte & Mackay, ring ☎ 01496 820240 for visiting information. There is a visitor centre and a shop.

The other big influence on the local economy is deer and the sporting estates. Jura has 6,000 deer give or take a few, and several estates cater for the sporting side of venison production. Salmon are also reared here at Inver, but the young fish are sold on.

Jura, unusually for its size, does not have a direct ferry link with the mainland, but despite its small population, under 200 people, it is a popular destination. George Orwell came here to recover from TB in 1947-48, completing his *1984* at Barnhill in the far northern end of the island. It is now available as a holiday let.

Passing yachts find Craighouse (or Small Isles) Bay a popular place to shelter for the night. Between the north end of Jura and the Isle of Scarba lies the Gulf of Corryvrecken (see also p.81-2). It has a dangerous whirlpool and is best avoided.

The village of Craighouse 8 miles/13km from the ferry has all the island's services plus the Jura Hotel, Jura stores, petrol, doctor's surgery etc.

The west coast has some remarkable examples of raised beaches. Once the Ice-Age glaciers melted, the land lifted up with the weight of the ice removed. This stranded the former coastline well above the current sea level.

The Whirlpool, Gulf of Corryvrecken

Fact File

Getting There

There is no direct ferry from the mainland for vehicles. You have to go to Port Askaig on Islay (see page 72) and get the short ferry from there to Feolin on Jura. There are frequent daily sailings. The 6.30pm ferry will wait for the Port Ellen bus which arrives at 6.35pm if asked for in advance. ☎ 01496 840681 Excellent views (weather permitting) from the ferry of Glas Bheinn and Dubha Bheinn (two large conical mountains, part of the Paps of Jura), each rising to over 1,700 ft/515m.

Islay Sea Safari

☎ 07768 450000/01496 840510
e: sailings@islayseasafari.co.uk
A new ferry has been introduced for foot traffic, which cuts two hours off the crossing time from the mainland. It runs from Tayvallich (on the mainland), situated near the head of Loch Sween and within one hour, crosses the Sound of Jura and lands you at Craighouse on Jura. At Tayvallich, ensure you park in the allocated area opposite the village hall. If possible, don't park in the street. Allow 5 minutes before departure for arrival. The ferry uses a 36 ft/11m RIB (Rigid Inflatable Boat) and the ferry is summer only (mid-June to September). It is daily except Wednesdays and there are four crossings each day.

Accommodation

Jura Hotel
Craighouse ☎ 01496 820243

Self-catering

Jura House, for up to 15 people, C/o Mirjam Cool, Cabrach, Craighouse, PA60 7XX
☎ 01496 820315

Burrbank Cottage, Craighouse
☎ 01496 820396

Boiden Cottage, Ardfarnal
☎ 01496 820393

Jura Holiday Let, Craighouse
☎ 01785 614701

Braeside, Craighouse
☎ 0141 946 4361

B&B

The Whitehouse, Ardfarnal
☎ 01496 820393

8 Woodside, Craighouse
☎ 01496 820319

The Manse, Craighouse
☎ 01496 820384

Places to Visit

Jura House & Gardens

The house was built in the early 1800s and is now available to let. The gardens, warmed by the Gulf Stream and sheltered by trees and shrubs, are host to many exotic plants, including a contingent from Australia which arrived in 1999. In summer, teas are available and there are two trails in the grounds. Off shore may be seen Heather Island and the ruins of Claig Castle.
Grounds open daily 9am-5pm; teas, weekdays in June-August.

Feolin Centre

Feolin Ferry House, PA60 7XX
Open: daily
Conducts research on Jura and boasts the largest documentation on the island. It has an exhibition on Jura.

Walking/Guided Tours

There are lots of opportunities; remember to watch out for golden eagles, deer stalkers and also adders. There is a minibus (the Jura Bus) up the only road (on the east coast) from Feolin to Ardlussa in the north. It runs daily (except Sunday). If you have left your car behind, it's a good substitute. ☎ 01496 820314. If you intend walking on the island, remember that deer stalking takes place from 1st July to 15th February. Contact local estates for information. If you are going into the Paps Region, call the Hillphone Service ☎ 01496 820151.

For a wildlife guided tour by a 12-seater Landrover, contact Mike Richardson on ☎ 07899 912116. He also has a B&B at Kinuachdrachd PA60 7XW

The Argyll Islands Tourist Guide Association also has qualified guides available.

Events

The Festival of Malts & Music, May
Fell Race, May
Jura Regatta, August
Plus lots of social events

Jura Bike Hire
☎ 07092 180747

Jura Distillery, Craighouse PA60 7XT
☎ 01496 820344
info@isleofjura.com
The distillery has 'The Lodge' available as holiday accommodation; also a 4-day residential course on the distillery and island life.

Colonsay and Oronsay

Colonsay

Colonsay is one of the smaller inhabited Inner Hebridean Islands, with the even smaller Oronsay lying off its southern coastline. Colonsay is 15 miles south of Mull and has a population of just over 100 people. It boasts many stunning sandy beaches with Kiloran Bay the most impressive, being over a mile long. The beaches are complimented by the cliffs on the west coast, the habitat of a large variety of seabirds. There are a variety of inland habitats too, with wild goats (traditionally stranded here after an Armada shipwreck) and more illusively, the otter.

Colonsay enjoys a mild climate, like neighbouring islands, and long hours of sunshine. It has a sand dune and machair (grassland) shoreline similar to that found in the Outer

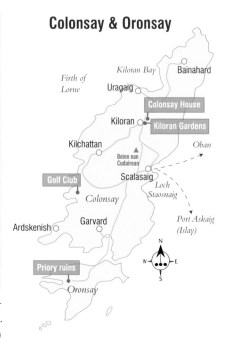

Colonsay & Oronsay

Firth of Lorne · Kiloran Bay · Bainahard · Uragaig · Colonsay House · Kiloran · Kiloran Gardens · Kilchattan · Oban · Beinn nan Cudairean · Scalasaig · Loch Staosnaig · Golf Club · Colonsay · Port Askaig (Islay) · Ardskenish · Garvard · Priory ruins · Oronsay

Below: Kiloran Bay, Colonsay

Porpoises off Colonsay

Hebrides. Like many islands off the western coast of Scotland, there is evidence of early occupation with sites of Bronze Age hut circles, Iron Age forts, a Norse burial site at Kiloran Bay and a 14th century Augustinian Priory with a church dating from AD1400.

Oronsay

Connected to Colonsay at low tide, it is c. 3 miles/14 km long, covers about 2 sq miles and has a population of 5 (in 2001). It is connected by a 1 mile causeway, called The Strand, across sand and mud flats. If you visit Oronsay Priory, judge the tide well to allow for a three hour visit – an hour each way and an hour at the Priory, a 14th century ruined Augustinian foundation, situated adjacent to Oronsay Farm.

The island became a conservation area in 2007, along with South Colonsay to protect a colony of choughs and corncrakes. The island is farmed by the RSPB with management of the habits of these two birds in mind. There are other species present, including breeding waders, farmland birds and wintering geese, taking advantage of farm grassland, sand dunes, machair and heathland.

The Priory is probably on the site as the original 6th century cell and an early Celtic cross, cared on Iona survies here. Much of its cloister also survives along with a lot of carved slabs from the Middle Ages which were carved here.

Oronsay Priory

Note that low tide extends for about three hours, so it is important that you judge departure right to visit the Priory. Take any food and drink needed with you. Do check the times carefully and check with a local person if you can. Tide tables are posted at the CalMac office.

Fact File

Getting There

CalMac do not have a direct ferry to Colonsay. Boats leave Oban on Wednesdays from Kennacraig to Port Ascraig on Islay, with a connecting boat to Scalasaig on Colonsay. The Wednesday boat coincides with the change over of a lot of accommodation and so advance booking is advised.

Seafari run from Easdale on a Rigid Inflatable Boat (RIB) to Colonsay.
☎ 01852 300003. Also Roger Easton operates out of Port Askaig
☎ 01496 302459.
The Oban ferry takes 2.5 hours.

Accommodation

Colonsay Hotel & Restaurant
Scalasaig, PA61 7YP
☎ 01951 200 316
e: reception@thecolonsay.com

For self catering cottages, there is a wide range available. See www.colonsay.org.uk

B&B
The Hannah's B&B
4 Uragaig, Isle of Colonsay, Argyll PA61 7YT
☎ 01951 200 150
e: thehannahbandb@aol.com

Corncrake Cottage
Homefield Croft PA61 7YR
☎ 01951 200118
rhonarobinson@btinternet.com

Donmar, PA61 7YT
☎ 01951 200223

Dharma Cottage, Kilchattan PA61 7YR
☎ 01951 200141
Colonsay Estate
Plus Bothy, dormitories and twin rooms, Backpackers Lodge, and over 20 holiday cottages
Booking Office, Isle of Colonsay PA61 7YU
☎ 01951 200 312
e: colonsaycottages@dial.pipex.com

Places to Visit
Colonsay House
Has a 20 acre exotic garden, including palm trees. April-June is the best time to visit it. The woodland garden is open daily, all year. On Wednesdays and Fridays during the summer the formal gardens around the house are open. It has one of the finest collections of rhododendrons in Scotland.

Golf Course: over 200 years old, 18 holes. Welcomes day visitors, but book in advance. Join at Colonsay Hotel or Colonsay Estate Office.

Fishing – fresh water brown trout. You need to join the Colonsay Fly Fishing Association (nominal amount) at Colonsay Hotel or Colonsay Estate office.

Events
Colonsay Gathering – March.
Ceol Cholasa (Folk Festival) – September.

Shopping

Scalasaig, PA61 7YR

☎ 01951 200 266

e: info@colonsayshop.net

Order your needs before you visit.

The Service Point

☎ 01951 200 263

Open Mon–Fri 9.30am - 12.30pm.
Includes the Library, office equipment you may need while on the island.

The Pantry

☎ 01951 200325

Licensed restaurant and tearoom, 100m from the pier. Gift shop and bakery

Colonsay oysters and honey

Andrew Abrahams, Pollgorm, Isle of Colonsay, Argyll, PA61 7YR

☎ 01951 200365,

e: colonsay.oysters.honey@dial.pipex.com

Colonsay has over half of all British wildflower species. The honey has a unique taste as a result. Honey and oysters available by mail order.

Colonsay Brewery, PA61 7YT

☎ 01951 200190

e: info@colonsaybrewery.co.uk

Mail order or direct to your boat.

Colonsay Naturally

4 Uragaig, Isle of Colonsay, Argyll PA61 7YT

☎ 01951 200150

Preserves, sauces, ketchups and chutneys.

There is a shop/PO, tea shop and also Church of Scotland and Baptist Churches. There is also a doctor on the island and a dispensing surgery.

Lismore

In the 13th century, Lismore became the seat of the bishopric of Argyll. Most of the cathedral was later demolished but the choir (? the chancel) survived. This was roofed in 1749 to serve as the parish church, which function it retains. The cathedral had previously been a monastery and the island, as a result, became a centre for Christianity from very early times. The church is dedicated to St. Moluag.

Consisting chiefly of limestone with basalt intrusions, the island boasts one such intrusion 70ft/21km high. Lismore is a long tongue of an island, 12miles/19km long and 1.5miles/2km wide. It has a raised beach, which is a feature common to several islands on the west coast. The island is very fertile, now supporting cattle and sheep and boasts a rich flora of some 300

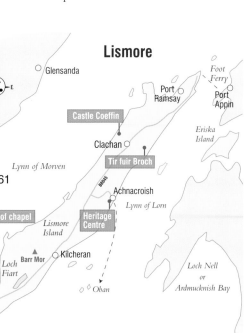

Lismore

species, with 130 bird species. The highest point is some 400 ft/122m high at Barr Mor.

Like most Scottish islands it was occupied in prehistoric times. There are 14 cairns, including Cnoc Aingeal, situated 3 miles/5km from the northern end of the island and the largest of its type in the region. From the Iron Age is a broch – Tir fuir. It is 15ft/4.5m high with 10ft/3mm walls, which incorporate an internal passageway. It is situated near to Balnagown Croft. There are the remains of Castle Coeffin, built on a Viking fort by the MacDougalls of Lorn.

Today the island has a population of c. 180.

Fact File

Getting There

Oban – Achnacroish operated by CalMac, 50 minutes.
From Port Appin, 6-minute foot ferry operated by Argyll & Bute Council.

Accommodation

Chiefly B&B/guesthouses and self-catering. Most are in the northern half of the island.
See isleoflismore.com

Places to Visit

Gaelic Heritage Museum
Port a Charron PA34 5UL
Consists of an award winning, new

museum, exhibition rooms and shop
☎ 01631 760030
Open: 11am-4pm. Winter opening by arrangement. Children free (< 16 years)
Incorporates the Lismore Café
(☎ 01631 760020) and the Tigh Iseabal Dhaidh, a traditional 19th century thatched cottage, open in summer.
(☎ 01631 760257)

Achandun Castle
Built by the Bishops of Argyll in the 13th century; remains only

Lismore Parish Church
A portion of the early monastery, restores in 1749

Facilities

Bike hire ☎ 01631 760213
Also at Port Appin ☎ 01631 730391

Post bus – 4 seat; available from the Post Office.

Taxi ☎ 01631 760220

There is no petrol available on Lismore.

Horse and carriage rides, runs from the passenger ferry to the museum.
☎ 01631 760393

Shop/Post Office ☎ 01631 760272
Closed Sundays

Mogwaii Design – products from pure wool.

Lismore lighthouse, Sound of Mull

Restaurant (at Port Appin, on the nearby mainland, via passenger ferry) Pier House Hotel, Seafood Restaurant, Port Appin, Argyll PA36 4DE
☎ 01631 730302

Seahorse crafts, pottery, designer bags etc.
Port Appin, ☎ 01631 730000

Kerrera

This island's north eastern point sits just off Oban. The island extends to nearly 5 miles/8km in length and is about 1.5 miles/2km in breadth. It rises to 612 ft/186m at Carn Breugach. The island is where the Scottish King Alexander II (1198 – 1249) died as he was about to invade the Outer Hebrides to oust the Viking occupation.

The island is reached by a passenger ferry from Gallanach on the coast road south west of Oban. Only residents' cars are allowed on the island. A circular path of 6 miles/10km around the southern part of the island is a good introduction to the island and takes in

Kerrera

Gylen Castle. This was a tower house built by 1587 and burnt by the Covenanters in 1647. The latter supported The Covenant of 1643. This was apparently to 'protect the liberty of an exposed site, a consolidated ruin and a far flung victim of tumultuous times' of long ago.

The current population is c. 30 people.

Fact File

Getting There

Kerrera Ferry
Daily from Gallanach Road, 1.5 miles/2km south west of Oban on coast road; summer: regular ferries and approximately every half hour in mid day ☎ 01631 563665 Passenger ferry only. All sailings are on request. To request ferry from the mainland, turn the white board to display the black side. Ferry bus runs May-Sept from Oban. It is the 431 and the 10.30am and the 4pm connect with the ferry. There is a car park north of Gallanach.

Accommodation

Kerrera Bunkhouse
☎ 01631 570223
17th century, sleeps up to 7 people. Two double bunks and separate sleeping platform for a double and single bed.

Places to Visit

Kerrera Tea Garden
Kerrera PA34 4SX
Open: Easter-Sep, 10.30am-4.30pm
☎ 01631 570223

Gylen Castle
Built 1582-57 by Duncan McDougal
3 miles/5km walk from Kerrera ferry

Slate Islands

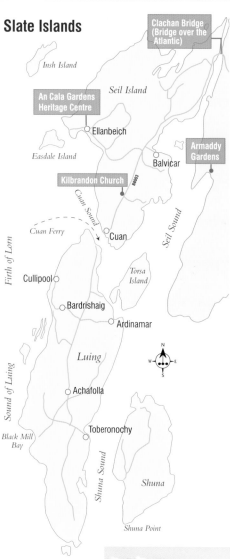

Insh Island

Seil Island

Clachan Bridge (Bridge over the Atlantic)

An Cala Gardens Heritage Centre

○ Ellanbeich

Easdale Island

Armaddy Gardens

Balvicar ○

Kilbrandon Church

B8003

Cuan Sound

Cuan Ferry

Cuan ↓

Cullipool ○

Torsa Island

Bardrishaig ○

Ardinamar ○

Firth of Lorn

Seil Sound

Luing

N
W—E
S

Achafolla ○

Sound of Luing

Toberonochy ○

Black Mill Bay

Shuna Sound

Shuna

Shuna Point

Luing

Situated at the Argyll coast are the four Slate Islands; Luing, Scarba, Seil and Shuna.

The largest is Luing, being immediately to the south of Seil and across the Sound of Shuna from the island of that name. It is 6 miles/9km long by 1.5m/2.4km and rises to 302 ft/92m high. It is composed of slate and a small amount of igneous rock (basalt). Seil is connected to the mainland by the graceful shingle arched bridge popularly known as the Bridge over the Atlantic. It as built in 1793 and is correctly known as the Clachan Bridge. It is therefore possible to get across Seil by car to North Cuan for the ferry to Luing.

The slate industry lasted from the late-Victorian period until 1965. The two villages of Cullipool and Toberonochy both had quarries, the slate leaving the island from the jetty at Black Mill Bay. In 1901 there were c.600 living on the island compared to the 200 or so now. With the end of slate extraction, the island's economy centres around agriculture and fishing, especially for lobsters, prawns and scallops. Look out for the Luing breed of cattle, a highland and shorthorn cross, recognised formally in 1965.

The island is attractive, but the number of attractions are limited owing to its size. You

Firth of Lorn
– Insh Isle

can get around the island on the Post bus, details from the post office at Cullipool. This doubles up as the island store for provisions and local crafts (coffee also available adjacent); ☎ 01852 314243. There are a couple of ruined hillforts from the Bronze Age and the ruins of Kitchattan Chapel. It was first recorded in 1589 and used until 1685.

Like the adjacent islands, the wildlife offers the chance of seeing seals, otters and various raptors including eagles. The island is near the Firth of Lorn Marine Conservation area, situated between Luing and Mull.

Fact File

Getting There

Ferry from North Cuan (on island of Seil), every 30 minutes during the daytime. There is a bus from Oban to North Cuan. The ferry carries 6 cars and 40 passengers across Cuan Sound.

Accommodation

Creagard House
48, Cullipool PA34 4UB
Quarry workers cottage, sleeps 6-7
☎ 0141 639 4592
e: cullypettigrew@hotmail.com

Two self-catering cottages
Cullipool
☎ 01852 314300

Breadalbane Cottage, Achafolla
Modernised 3 bedroom cottage.
www.bookcottages.com

The Bothy
Bardrishaig
2 bedroom cottage
☎ 01852 314388

8, Cullipool
One large bedroom
☎ 07708 322929

Torsa House and Island House
The only property on the island of Torsa (adjacent to Luing).
Sleeps 4-5.
Includes use of boat. Torsa is owned by the Armaddy Estate.
It is north east of Luing in Seil Sound.
☎ 01852 314274
e: torsa@btinternet.com

Sunnybrae Caravan Park PA34 4TU
Seven waterfront mobile homes
☎ 01852 314274
e: sunnybrae_living@btinternet.com

Places to Visit

The Scottish Slate Islands Heritage Trust has a museum on adjacent Easdale Island (off Seil Island).

Scarba

Situated to the south west of Luing Island and 1.5m miles/2 km north of Jura is Scarba, one of the slate islands. Today, occupation here is confined to Kilmory Lodge, a shooting lodge of the island's owner and Bagh Gleam a'Mhaoil in the south, now an outward bound centre.

This small island is 3.5m/6km in length and just over that in width. Cruach Scarba rises to c. 1,470 ft/448m and is pyramidal in shape. Much of it is heather covered or forested, supporting red deer, wild goats and otters. There is some grazing for sheep from Luing. On the east side there are the ruins of crofts and a chapel.

Between Scarba and Jura is the Gulf of Corryvreckan. At certain times of the year, there is a noticeable imbalance in the level of the sea either side of the islands. This creates a strong tidal stream which may be dangerous, creating a

Scarba & Lunga

whirlpool said to be the world's third largest.

The West Coast of Scotland Pilot states 'When the tidal streams jet through the gulf, navigation at times is very dangerous and no vessel should then attempt this passage without local knowledge. The passage through, from west to east is not so risky as that in the opposite direction.'

Seil Island

Seil is situated adjacent to the Argyll mainland. It is so close that it has been joined by the Clachan Bridge since 1793 (The Bridge over the Atlantic).

The island is 4.25m/7km by 2.25m/3.6km and rises to 474 ft/144m at Meall in height. Beyond it are the Luing and Shuna islands and further out into the Firth of Lorn are Scarba,

The Bridge over the Atlantic, Seil

Lunga and the Garvellach Islands. Mull is 4m/6km to the north west. Slate was formerly worked here (see below). West of Balvicar, the island changes its character: cultivation is less and the area has a moorland look about it.

Slate was worked on the adjacent and much smaller island of Easdale since before the mid 16th Century and lasted on Seil until 1881, with a subsequent revival between the 1940s and 60s. The roof of Iona Abbey is covered with Seil slate. The two islands (Seil and Easdale) plus Luing and Belnahua comprise a loose grouping known as the Slate Islands, although Shuna, Scarba and Kerrera also have a claim to the name.

Belnahua is situated 1.5m/2km north west of Luing and west of Seil Island. It has no resident population now and is scarred from slate quarrying. It is privately owned. The island rises to a height of 70 ft/21m and has a jetty on its east side.

For map see p.81

Fact File
Getting There
Ferry to Easdale (from Ellenabeich) Passenger only, operated by Argyll & Bute Council daily.
First and last ferry needs to be booked with ferryman by noon on previous days.
☎ 01631 562 125
The Council also operates the Cuan to Luing Island vehicle ferry.

Accommodation
Bed and Breakfast
Garraghmhor
Ellenabeich, Easdale, Seil Island PA34 4RF
☎ 01852 300513

Innish B&B
Clachan Bridge, Seil Island
☎ 01852 300423

Tigh an Truish Inn
Clachanseil, Seil Island PA34 4QZ
☎ 01852 300242

22 Easdale Island ☎ 01852 300438
Mutiara, Clachanseil ☎ 01852 300241
(May–Sept)

Self Catering
There is a lot of choice, go to www.seil.oban.ws/selfcatering

Places to Visit
The Heritage Centre, Ellenabeich

Kilbrandon Church
for its stained glass windows.

An Cala Gardens
Ellenabeich, Seil
Highland Arts Exhibition, Easdale, Ellenabeich PA34 4RQ
☎ 01852 300273

Other Attractions
Boat Trips/Kayaks
Seafari Adventures
Ellenabeich, Easdale, Argyll PA34 4RQ
☎ 01852 300003
Trips to Iona; Garvellach Islands (for wildlife tours); Belnahua Islands (the most remote of the Slate Islands – abandoned c. 1915); Gulf of Corryvreckan – world's third largest whirlpool. If you are lucky you should see whales and basking sharks.

Sealife Adventures from Balvicar
☎ 01631 571010 (office hours)
e: info@sealife-adventures.com
Two five-hour cruises available

Sea Kayak Hire
Balvicar
☎ 01852 300589

Eating Out

On Seil – Tigh & Truish Inn, ☎ 01852 300242; Oyster Bar & Restaurant, Balvicar ☎ 01852 300121. Puffer Bar, Easdale, ☎ 01852 300022

Fishing

Permits available in Oban. Boatyard, Balvicar ☎ 01852 300557

Golf

Isle of Seil Golf Course – 9 holes.

Local Produce

Easdale Seafoods ☎ 01852 300295

Tourist Information Office, Oban
☎ 01631 563122
e: info@oban.org. uk

Nearby Mainland Gardens

Armaddy Castle Garden
Nr. Caddleton, Nr. Oban PA34 4QY
☎ 01852 300 353
Open 9am – dusk daily
Rhododendrons and woodland walk.
self-catering cottages.

Angus's Gardens
Barguillean Farm, Glen Lonan, Taynuilt, Argyll PA35 1HY
☎ 01866 822 333
Situated east of Oban. 9 Acre woodland garden with lake. There is a self-catering cottage here.

Arduaine Gardens
On the A816, adjacent to the coast, midway between Oban and Lochgilphead on the Loch Fyne coast. National Trust for Scotland PA34 4XQ
Open 9.30am – sunset daily
☎ 0844 4932216
20 acres of woodland plants. Entrance shared with Loch Melfort Hotel.

Shuna Island

Shuna is situated 1.5 miles/3 km off the Craignish Peninsula on the Argyll mainland, separated by Loch Shuna from the mainland and by Shuna Sound to the west, from the island of Luing. Shuna rises to a height of 290 ft/88 m at Druim na Dubh Ghlaic. It measures 1.25 miles/2 km x 2.5 miles/4 km.

The island has no roads and no cars are permitted. There is some woodland, giving cover for red, roe and fallow deer. Shuna Castle was built as late as 1911 at lavish expense but is now a ruin. The island is privately owned and the sensitive ecology and wildlife are protected, with a strategy of maximising bio-diversity and sustainability. Visitors are free to explore the island.

Location map p.80

Fact File

Accommodation

Shuna Farm Cottages
 The Farmhouse, Isle of Shuna, Arduaine, Argyll PA34 4SZ
☎ 01852 314244
e:info@islandofshunaco.uk.
Cottages are available with idyllic locations.

Access from the mainland is from the village of Craobh Haven, off the A816, north north west of Kilmarten. The village was established in 1993 and consists of some 30 houses with three shops and The Lord of the Isles pub/restaurant, which also has accommodation. The address is Craobh Haven, Arduaine, Argyll, PA31 8UA, ☎ 01852 500658. The village is popular as a yachting marina. Cruises around The Slate Islands are run from Croabh Haven by Farsain Cruises. Just to the north of Craobh Haven (2miles/3km) the National Trust for Scotland manages Arduaine Gardens (see p.84).

Do not confuse this island with Shuna Island in Loch Linnhe, north of Oban.

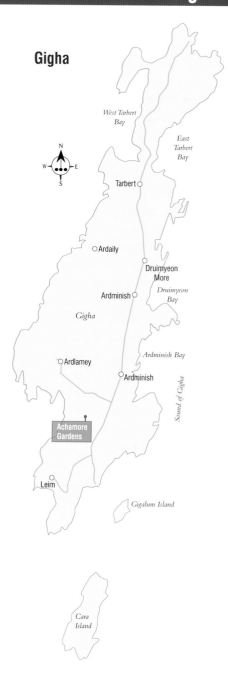

Gigha

This island, pronounced 'Gear' is three miles west of the Kintyre coast. It is 7 miles long and 1.5 miles wide. 100 years ago, the population was 370, but is now c.120 people. It gets its name from the Viking word 'Gudey' meaning the good isle, and indeed it is. It is favoured by a climate that is drier and warmer than is usual in that area and benefits from more than average sunshine.

In 2002, the islanders purchased the island, together with Achamore House and gardens. The island and gardens are now owned by the Isle of Gigha Heritage Trust. The house was sold on to help cover the purchase cost. The latter was built in 1884 in baronial-style and was designed by a firm employing the then young Charles Rennie Macintosh, one of Scotland's greatest architects. It is claimed that he had some influence over the design, which may still be seen.

In 1944 the island and house was purchased by Sir James Horlick, who created a 50 acre garden, now farmed for its rare plants, including many rhododendrons, trees and shrubs. Some of these are sub-tropical, but grow well in the protected gardens, taking advantage of the climate here.

The gardens are open to the public and the house now has 11 bedrooms to let (Achamore House, Isle of Gigha, Argyll, Scotland PA41 7AD ☎ 01583 505400 e: gigha@atlas.co.uk)

The house also runs sea tours to neighbouring islands and even over to Ballycastle in Northern Ireland, plus Oban etc. They will also pick up from Tayinloan if at least two of you have missed the ferry. (Gigha Sea Tours, ☎ 01583 505404, info@gighaseatours.co.uk). The boat is a 12m catamaran.

The island also has a nine-hole golf course near to Achamore House. The island is also good to explore and you are promised views of seals and otters on the shoreline. There are white, unspoilt sandy beaches at Ardminish, Leim and Druimyeon More.

Fact File

Getting There

CalMac run the Gigha ferry from Tayinloan. It takes 20 minutes and boats leave Tayinloan regularly through to tea time. There are later boats in the summer season. There is no service 25th December and 1st January and a Sunday service operates on the day following these two days. Caravans are not permitted on Gigha. Latest check in time is 10 minutes prior to departure across the Sound of Gigha to Ardminish.

Accommodation

Gigha Hotel
Isle of Gigha, Argyll, PA41 7AA
☎ 01583 505254
e: hotel@gigha.org.uk
Claims to be the UK's first community-owned hotel.
Also 6 self catering cottages around the island.

Achamore House
see across

Post Office Guest House
B&B and self-catering
☎ 01583 505251

Tighnavinish (B&B)
☎ 01583 505378

9, Ardminish (self-catering)
☎ 01546 603650

Campsite adjacent to the Boathouse. Check availability on arrival on
☎ 01583 505123.

Facilities

Boathouse Café and Bar
Meals and drinks throughout the day
Shop and PO nearby.

Gigha has a music festival in early September.

Gigalum & Cara Islands
These lie to the south, with Gigalum nearest to Gigha. There is one house on Gigalum and it is eight-sided. Cara is larger (1 mile x 0.5 mile), lying a mile or so south of Gigha. There is no ferry service to either, but Gigha Seatours run trips around both islands.

Arran

Arran is the largest of the seven islands in the Firth of Clyde. It extends some 20 miles/32km from north to south and is 8–10.5 miles/13–17km wide, covering 165 sq. miles. It is a popular destination for ramblers and climbers and its rugged mountains afford fantastic views. In addition to the tourist trade, agriculture (cattle and sheep) is important. Fishing for herring was also important until the fish moved elsewhere. Off the south east coast is Holy Island, now a Buddhist Retreat, which offers accommodation to visitors.

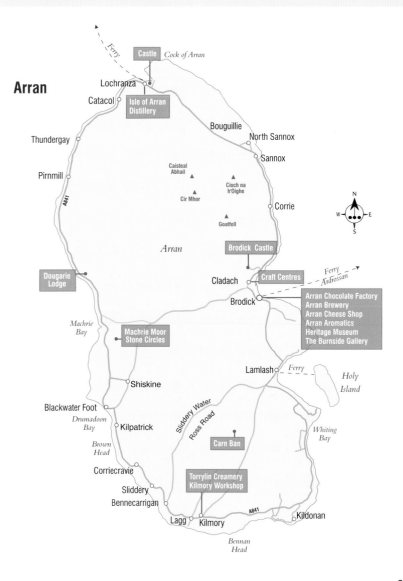

Standing stones, Machrie Moor

Brodick Castle

Brodick is the main town and where many of the attractions are located (other than the countryside and the mountains). There is a brewery, chocolate factory, cheese factory and Arran Aromatics, who make handmade soaps and other beauty products. The Heritage Centre has extensive galleries and is close to Brodick Castle, which dates from the 14th Century. It is the oldest habitable property owned by the National Trust for Scotland. It is richly furnished and has lovely gardens.

There are 14 villages on the island including Lochranza in the north, which has a ferry connection to Kintyre, and a distillery.

Fact File

Getting There

CalMac Ferry from Ardrossan to Brodick, 55 mins. Latest check in time, vehicles 30 mins, passengers 10 mins. Aslo from Claonaig (Kintyre) to Lochranza, 30 mins. Latest check in time, vehicles and passengers 10 mins. Bookings ☎ 08705 650000. Bus Services on Arran ☎ 0870 6082608.

Tourist Information Centre

The Pier Head, Brodick
☎ 01770 302140

Attractions

Arran Heritage Museum
Brodick
☎ 01770 302636
Open daily, April – Oct. 10.30am–4pm

Arran Brewery
Home Farm, Brodick
☎ 01770 302353
Open: Summer Mon–Sat, 10am-5pm, Sun 12.30pm-5pm, Winter (late Sept–Easter closed Sun and Tues), 10am-3.30pm
Situated adjacent to the castle

Balmichael Visitor Centre
Shiskine
☎ 01770 860430
Craft studios, gift shops

Brodick Castle (NT)
☎ 01770 302202
Open daily April - October

Isle of Arran Distillery
Lochranza
☎ 01770 830264
Open March – December, daily in summer.
One of the few remaining independent Scottish distillers

Crafts and produce of Arran

Arran Aromatics
Home Farm, Brodick KA27 8DD
☎ 01770 302873

Arran Cheese Shop
Home Farm, Brodick KA27 8DD
☎ 01770 302788
Open all year.

Arran Chocolate Factory
Brodick
☎ 01770 302873

Paterson Arran Ltd
The Old Mill, Lamlash, KA27 8AR
☎ 01770 600606
Open all year.
Kitchen & Farm Shop. Sells a range of Arran products, from marmalade to mustards made with Arran whisky and chutney with Arran beer.

Tonylin Creamery
Kilmory
☎ 01770 870240

Pony Trekking

Cairn House
Blackwaterfoot
☎ 01770 860466

Machrie Bay Stables
☎ 0047 40 222923

North Sannox
☎ 01770 810222

Cycle Hire

Brodick Cycles
Opposite the village hall
☎ 01770 302460

Golf

There are 7 golf courses on Arran (4 with 18 holes). See www.scottishgolfsouthwest.com

Guide Book: *Landmark Visitors Guide, Arran, Bute and Cumbrae* by Ron Scholes.

Glencloy Water to Goatfell

Bute

Another of the seven islands in the Firth of Clyde, it has snuggled up against the mainland, separated by the Kyles of Bute, at its northern end. In fact it is only a short distance from Colintraive.

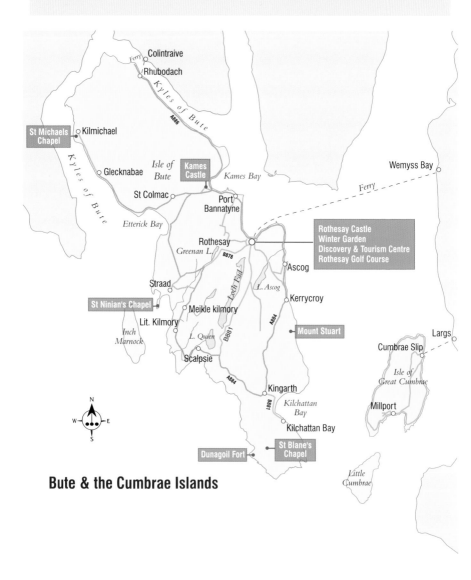

Bute & the Cumbrae Islands

Kerrycroy, Bute

Rothesay Castle, Bute

and is noted for its scenery. In fact there are memorable views all around the island, especially along much of the coastline.

The climate is mild, being sheltered by Arran and the Kintyre peninsula. There are three significant gardens open to the public – see Attractions below.

Fact File

Getting There

CalMac Ferry from Wemyss Bay to Rothesay, 35 mins. Latest check in – vehicles 30 mins, passengers 10 mins. Daily, but not 25th December and 1st January
Also from Colintraive to Rhubodach, daily, check in 5 mins. Latest check in time – vehicles and passengers 5 mins. Trains from Glasgow Central to Wemyss Bay. From airports catch train at Paisley.
Bute is one of the easiest islands to reach, particularly if you are travelling north.

It is about 15.5 miles/25km long and is nowhere as wide as 6 miles10km from coast to coast. The main town is Rothesay, which still has its castle, which is believed to date from the 12th century. Perhaps the main visitor attraction is Mount Stuart, the home of the Marquis of Bute. The family made its fortune in the coal trade at Cardiff. This Gothic Revival-style building, its lovely grounds and some magnificent treasures within the house, attracts c.30,000 visitors a year. It is built on the site of a previous house destroyed by fire in 1877. There is a lot to see here.

Bute has the advantage of lovely countryside close to the mainland. It also is protected rather well by Arran and the Kyle of Lochalsh and therefore has a more sheltered climate. In addition to the usual seals, which frequent this coast, keep a weather eye out for submarines coming from or heading for Holy Loch. The semi-circular coastline fronting the Kyles of Bute in the north is 16 miles/26km long

Accommodation

Full details from Tourist Information, 15, Victoria Street, Rothesay PA20 0AJ
☎ 08707 200619/01700 502151.
Info@rothesay.visitscotland.com

Attractions

Ardencraig Gardens and Aviary
High Craigmore PA20 9EZ
☎ 01700 504644
Open May – Sept.

Ascog Hall Fernery & Gardens
☎ 01700 504555
Open Easter to end of October

Mount Stuart

Bute Museum
☎ 01700 505067
Open all year

Mount Stuart House & Gardens
☎ 01700 503877
www.mountstuart.com
Open Easter & May – Sept.

Rothesay Castle
☎ 01700 502691
Open all year

Rothesay Discovery Centre
☎ 01700 502151

Kingarth Pony Trekking
Kilchattan Bay
☎ 01700 831673

Golf Course
18 holes, Rothesay
☎ 01700 503554

Doctor ☎ 01700 502290

Bus Services: ☎ 01546 6004360

Guidebook: *Landmark Visitors Guide Arran, Bute and Cumbrae* by Ron Scholes.

Great and Little Cumbrae

The two islands are situated between the southern part of Bute and the mainland. There is a ferry to Cumbrae Slip on Gt. Cumbrae from Largs (CalMac). Both islands are small, Gt. Cumbrae's road around the coast being only 10.5 miles/17 km long. The island is great for cycling, the preferred option of many visitors. Millport, on the south coast, has the Cathedral of the Isles, opened in 1851 and Britain's smallest cathedral.

For the active, the Scottish National Water Sports Centre is based at Cumbrae Slip. Cycles may be hired in Millport and the town also boasts sandy beaches and safe bathing.

Cumbrae Voyages offer 'unforgettable marine adventures and wildlife tours' amongst the lower Clyde islands. They use 12-seater rigid inflatable boats and operate on any day subject to a minimum number of 8 booked. If you are lucky there are occasional sightings of porpoise, dolphins and whales. They also offer land-based adventure activities with mountain bikes, quad bikes, etc.

Little Cumbrae

The island is privately owned and public access is not generally available.

Fact File

Getting There

Largs – Cumbrae Slip (Gt Cumbrae). Daily latest check-in time, vehicles and passengers, 10 mins. No service 25th December or 1st January. Bus from Cumbrae Slip to Milltown.

Accommodation

For somewhere unusual, the Grade A listed college next to the Cathedral has rooms available, with half and full board terms also available. ☎ 01475 530353.

Tourist Information

Attractions etc

Cumbrae Voyages
☎ 0845 2570404
From Millport Pier

Cathedral of the Isles
☎ 01475 530353

Cycle Hire
Millport
☎ 01475 540478

Golf
18 holes ☎ 01475 530306

Doctor
☎ 01465 530329

Guide Book: *Landmark Visitors Guide Arran, Bute and Cumbrae* by Ron Scholes.

Ailsa Craig

Guarding the entrance to the Clyde like a massive block-house is the dramatic shape of this uninhabited island. Its sides rise sheer out of the water and above them, from a distance, the profile is of an inverted cone rising to a point. The island is all that remains of the core of a former volcano. Today it is a site of special scientific interest and is the home of 73,000 breeding seabirds of which nearly half are gannets. The rest are chiefly guillemots and black guillemots, razor bills and puffins. The latter have thrived since the resident brown rat population was eradicated.

There used to be a lighthouse keeper here and the former granite quarry swelled the population to 29 at the end of the Victorian era, but by 1904, it was down to nine people. It was this small community that inadvertently introduced the rats. They obviously liked the place and by 1934 had wiped out the puffins.

The lighthouse was built in 1886 by Thomas Stevenson and his nephew David. Thomas was the father of Robert Louis Stevenson, the writer. Now the lighthouse is automated. The quarry was closed too but supplied riebeckite, a black volcanic stone for building stones (eg on the floor of the Chapel of the Thistle, St. Giles Cathedral, Edinburgh). Another more unusual use was for curling stones, including those used by the Scottish Womens' team when they won the gold medal at the Winter Olympics in 2002.

There are no formal arrangements about landing and to view the birds at their best, there is no need to land. The RSPB has managed a reserve here since 2004 and do not permit dogs to land except registered guide dogs. The island is known as Paddy's Milestone, being halfway between Belfast and Glasgow.

It is 10 miles/16km west of Girvan and can be easily seen on a clear day as it rises to 1,114ft/338m in height. The lighthouse faces Girvan and is adjacent to the ruins of the castle keep. Prior to the introduction of wireless telegraph in 1935, pigeons and even fires were used to summon assistance from the mainland.

Fact File

Getting There

From Girvan: There are daily summer sailings:
Kintyre Express ☎ 01294 270160 and Mark McCrindle ☎ 01465 713219
(e: mccrindle@aol.com/
w: www.ailsacraig.org.uk)

From Campbeltown:
Mull of Kintyre Seatours
☎ 07785 542811

From Gt Cumbrae (Millport Pier):
Cumbrae Voyages ☎ 0845 257 0404
(they also operate out of Largs).

It is possible to land but there are no facilities if you do so. Access is from the north east side.

Index